Collaborate
Move•Meant

A contextual guide to life with Jesus

Donovan Dreyfus

ISBN-10: 1490456295
ISBN-13: 978-1490456294

CONTENTS

ACKNOWLEDGMENTS

I am grateful for all of the people who have taken the time to hear my heart and encourage me to write the *Collaborate Move•Meant* guide. Your caring input has always been given when it was needed the most.

Thank you mom for your passion and commitment to writing throughout your lifetime. Your love for writing has influenced me to fulfill my God-given calling of completing this guide.

I also wish to remember my dad, Terry Vaughn Dreyfus, who passed away in 2006. Opportunities that he created for me led to the completion of this guide.

Thank you Mr. and Mrs. LaFlamme for taking me into your family as a spiritual son and mentoring me in the ministry. You two have been the greatest spiritual influence in my life.

Finally, thank you Alex Haselden and Carlos Kokinda for reviewing the text and offering helpful suggestions for the guide.

PREFACE

Collaborate Move•Meant is a brief contextual guide to life with Jesus. The content of this guide is placed within three spiritually moving contexts. The Sacrificial, Positional, and Experiential contexts work together, side by side, to offer a compelling message of God's love and life with Jesus.

A collaborate with Jesus section, testimonial, and prayer is at the end of every part to enhance each context. Also, most of the supporting scriptural content is limited to the writings of the Apostles John and Paul for easy cross-reference with the Bible.

Lastly, a personal profile and affirmations section is included to make the *Collaborate Move•Meant* guide a perfect companion book for life's spiritual journey.

Jesus collaborator,

Donovan Dreyfus
collaboratemovemeant.com
facebook.com/CollaborateMoveMeant

INTRODUCTION

"(You) have made us kings and priests to our God; and let us reign on the earth." (Revelation 5:10 NKJV)

After receiving ministry from the team, I struggled to make my way to the chair. God's presence was so strong on me; I could barely walk to my place without falling over. Surrounded by the love of Jesus, I sat in His presence as He whispered into my ear. He spoke truth and life into me for some time. He directly spoke to me saying, "I crown you." Then, He spiritually placed a crown on my head. It was my very own personalized commission from Jesus to carry out His kingdom work on Earth. I will never forget the day Jesus placed a crown on my head.

How would you view yourself differently after being crowned as royalty for the rest of your life? Imagine having kingdom status and power to triumphantly rule on the Earth. What changes would you make in the world?

The Bible reveals that God lovingly created humanity to reciprocate His love and reign with Him in all of the world. The first two people God breathed life into were Adam and Eve. Adam and Eve walked and talked with God in the Garden of Eden. They ruled over all creation in the splendid paradise. The only restriction God gave them was not to eat from the tree of the knowledge of good and evil. God warned them of the death they would fatally experience if they did so.

Unfortunately, satan (purposely not capitalized) deceived Adam and Eve into tasting the forbidden fruit. As a result, they experienced an immediate spiritual death and an eventual physical death.

Although their spirits were dead due to sin, they continued to live in an altered spiritual condition with a corrupt soul and dying body. They also forfeited their regal right to rule over the glorious garden. Consequently, they were permanently expelled from Eden.

Our two-fold problem

We inherited Adam and Eve's dead spiritual condition within a dramatically different context. We were born into the world, not the paradise garden. Furthermore, we began life without having the experience of talking and walking with God, much less reigning with Him. We never experienced God as our life.

To our disadvantage, we were born into the world without the ability to spiritually live to God. We tragically inherited the two-fold problem of living to sin and dying to God. Our dead nature rendered us powerless to stop sinning and made us unable to avoid dying to God. Therefore, satan ruled over us through the power of sin and death (Romans 5:12).

Thankfully, we do not have to overcome this complex spiritual dilemma alone. God has supernaturally made a way for us to experience His love and live for Him through His Son, Jesus Christ.

Sacrificial context

God sent Jesus from heaven to live out the perfect example of reciprocating the Father's love and reigning with Him on the Earth. Jesus was conceived in the Virgin Mary through the supernatural work of the Holy Spirit (Luke 1:35). The Holy Spirit was with Jesus in heaven, accompanied Jesus to Earth, and present with Jesus in His birth. Therefore, Jesus was born into the world with a sinless spirit, or nature.

Although Jesus was tempted in every way as a man, He never lived to sin. Jesus wholeheartedly collaborated with His Father without submitting to satan's usurped rule on the Earth. Jesus faultlessly obeyed the Father's word spoken over Him, within Him, and through Him in all that He did and said. Even in the face of death, He obeyed His Father's will by offering Himself up as a sinless sacrifice on the cross. He laid down His life to pay the eternal penalty and debt for a sin-saturated humanity.

Positional context

There is much to learn from the life of Jesus leading up to the cross, but we also gain valuable insight from the supernatural event of the cross.

God wisely placed sinful humanity in the body of Jesus to be crucified with Him on the cross. Sinful humanity, with its dead nature, was spiritually crucified with Jesus. Humanity, including you and me, was spiritually buried with Jesus. Afterward, God resurrected humanity with a newly created spiritual nature that was united with the nature of Jesus. Finally, God positioned us to be seated next to His loving side in the heavenly places in Jesus.

The Biblical revelation of being crucified, buried, resurrected and seated with Jesus in the heavenly places are central truths of the message of Jesus. These central truths can become a set of core beliefs that enables followers of Jesus to reciprocate God's love and live to Him.

Experiential context

Since we died with Jesus, we can experience a new collaboration life with God. Our new spiritual life is in Jesus. Our new supernatural life is Jesus. By acting on revelation of the cross event, including the crucifixion, burial, resurrection, and enthronement of Jesus, we can die to sin. Through belief and faith in Jesus, as our life, we can supernaturally live to God. We also learn how to fulfill our God-given destiny of presently ruling on the Earth through Jesus as the Father's royal children.

Collaborate with Jesus

In essence, the *Collaborate Move•Meant* guide expressly declares, "God meant for Jesus to move us."

The Bible poignantly states, "By this the love of God was manifested in us, that God has sent His only begotten Son into the world so that we might live through Him" (1 John 4:9). We begin to experience God's perfect, passionate love for us when we embrace Jesus as our life. We continue to encounter our Father's manifest love toward us as we live out our God-given destiny through Jesus.

If you have never experienced Jesus as your life, begin collaborating with Him by praying the following prayer out loud. Your life will be forever changed as you experience His love, presence, and power to victoriously rule on the Earth. I promise, you will view yourself differently as royalty seated in the heavenly places.

Prayer

Thank you Jesus for freely offering yourself up on the cross for me. I fully agree that I am unable to stop sinning on my own. I am also unable to avoid dying to God because of my spiritual condition. I need to be awakened to your life in my spirit, soul, and body. Make my spirit alive in yours. Be my life Jesus!

Also, show me how to reciprocate with our Father's love and live to Him. I want to talk and walk with God every breathing moment of my new life in You.

Lastly, establish the truth of being crucified, buried, resurrected and enthroned with You as a set of core beliefs in my heart and mind. Enable me to act on the revelation of the cross. I choose to die to sin and live to God. Thank you Jesus, for teaching me how to collaborate with You and fulfill my God-given destiny.

PART ONE:
SACRIFICIAL CONTEXT

"Worthy is the Lamb that was slain to receive power and riches and wisdom and might and honor and glory and blessing!" (Revelation 5:12)

Jesus was publicly announced to Israel as the Lamb of God by their prophet John the Baptist. When Jesus came to him, the prophet boldly declared before the crowd, "Behold, the Lamb of God who takes away the sin of the world" (John 1:29)! He heard from his Father in heaven that Jesus was the sacrificial Lamb sent to Earth for the Jews. Jesus was immersed in the river for baptism and raised out of the water to fulfill His earthly destiny of being the Father's slain Lamb.

The slain Lamb

Interestingly, when God raised His Son from the dead, Jesus was enthroned in heaven as a slain Lamb (Revelation 5:6). He gloriously resurrected His Son to look like a sacrifice in heaven even though He had already been slain on Earth. Why would God leave marks from the crucifixion on His resurrected Son in heaven?

The Apostle John wrote about the slain Lamb that was worshiped by multitudes of angels and living creatures in the book of Revelation. He witnessed every creature in heaven and on Earth saying,

"To Him who sits on the throne, and to the Lamb, be blessing and honor and glory and dominion forever and ever!" (Revelation 5:13)

John repeatedly referred to Jesus as the slain Lamb ruling from His throne in heaven. In fact, the Lamb is used as a name for Jesus several more times than any other name (twenty-eight total) in the entire book of Revelation.

One intriguing statement that John made about Jesus in Revelation 13:8 states, "All who dwell on the earth will worship Him, whose names have not been written in the Book of Life of the Lamb slain from the foundation of the world" (NKJV). This verse sheds light on how the Lamb was predestined before the creation of the world to be slain for the sins of humanity. God planned out the sacrificial death of Jesus before the creation of the world to forever establish His kingdom reign on Earth.

Sacrificial nature of the Lamb

Jesus led a sacrificial life from His youth until the last breathing moment of His death on the cross. The cross of the Lamb was a graphic depiction of the sacrificial nature He inwardly possessed from all of eternity until He was physically slain. Every excruciating moment on the cross displayed the depths of His sacrificial heart toward His Father and humanity. Even still, the amount of pain and suffering He gruesomely endured did not equally express the measure of His sacrificial love.

Let's take a closer look at the earthly life of Jesus to identify the heart of the Lamb that sacrificed everything for His Father.

Sent from heaven

The apostle Paul gave an insightful account of the inner disposition of Jesus when He was sent from heaven to fulfill the Father's kingdom purpose on Earth. Apostle Paul stated that Jesus,

"Being in the form of God, did not consider it robbery to be equal with God, but made Himself of no reputation, taking the form of a bondservant, and coming in the likeness of men. And being found in

appearance as a man, He humbled Himself and became
obedient to the point of death, even the death of the cross."
(Philippians 2:6-8 NKJV)

Jesus unclothed Himself of His outward heavenly splendor to serve in the likeness of man. Even so, the glorious virtue of sacrificial obedience was marvelously displayed through His humanity.

Jesus laid down His eternal kingly stature to take on the likeness of a mortal man while remaining fully God. Jesus openly declared His deity by stating to God's chosen people in their temple, "Truly, truly, I say to you, before Abraham was born, I am" (John 8:58). Some of the religious leaders quickly tried to kill Jesus for making the claim of eternally existing before their patriarch and spiritual father Abraham was born.

Furthermore, He stated, "For if you believed in Moses, you would believe Me: for he wrote about Me. But if you do not believe his writings, how will you believe My words" (John 5:46). Jesus was making it clear to the Jews that their Scriptures gave witness to Him before He was born into the world (John 5:39).

Position in heaven while on Earth

As God in the flesh, Jesus was not of the world even though He was sent into the world. John the Baptist gave witness to Jesus occupying a place in heaven while walking on Earth by stating, "He who comes from above is above all; he who is of the earth is earthly and speaks of the earth. He who comes from heaven is above all" (John 3:31). Jesus openly told of His position in heaven saying, "No one has ascended to heaven but He who came down from heaven, that is, the Son of Man who is in heaven" (John 3:13 NKJV). Again, Jesus said, "You are from below, I am from above; you are of this world, I am not of this world" (John 8:23). During His time on Earth, Jesus lived from a heavenly orientation by virtue of His position in His heavenly Father. All of who Jesus was and what He was capable of doing originated from the kingdom of heaven, not from the world.

Jesus spiritually lived from His home in heaven through a thriving faith in His heavenly Father while physically dwelling on Earth.

Father's presence on Earth

Although Jesus was God in the flesh, it is vital to understand that He lived a life of faith as a man on the Earth. Jesus openly declared His life of faith in this way:

"When you lift up the Son of Man, then you will know that I am He, and that I can do nothing of Myself; but as My Father taught Me, I speak these things. And He who sent Me is with Me. The Father has not left Me alone, for I always do those things that please Him." (John 8:28-29 NKJV)

Jesus experienced God, the Father, as His life. In every breathing moment of His existence on Earth, He sacrificially lived to the Father to see what the Father was doing from heaven (John 5:19-20). With unwavering belief, He allowed God to author His life story throughout His entire faith journey. Jesus not only treasured and safeguarded the Father's word in His heart, but He also kept it by accomplishing what the Father commanded Him to do (John 8:55). As a man of faith, Jesus lived in complete dependence on the Father. Thus, He perfectly collaborated with the Father in all that He said and did.

Jesus also exercised an abiding faith that kept Him in the manifest presence of the Father on Earth. Jesus expressed His great faith in the Father by stating, "As the living Father sent Me, and I live because of the Father" (John 6:57). Again, Jesus said, "I am not alone, but I am with the Father who sent Me" (John 8:16 NKJV). Yet again, Jesus stated, "I and My Father are one" (John 10:30 NKJV). Jesus went on to say that the miraculous works He performed proved that the Father was present with Him and remained in Him (John 10:37-38).

The transfiguration experience of Jesus was the greatest expression of His heavenly orientation within the Father (Matthew 17:2). During the transfiguration, Jesus literally transformed from the Son of Man in the flesh into the Son of God in a glorified body. The glory radiating from Jesus brilliantly revealed His heavenly orientation within the Father. Then, God surrounded Jesus with His glory cloud. Immediately afterward, He audibly told the disciples to listen to His Son, in whom He was very pleased. During those magnificent moments, Jesus fully lived from His position in heaven while experiencing the Father's powerful manifest presence on Earth.

Self-glorification denied

The heart of the Lamb lived to glorify His Father, rather than Himself. Jesus sacrificially denied worldly self-glorification to remain an obedient Son.

According to the *New Oxford American Dictionary*, self-glorification is the exaltation of oneself and abilities. Had Jesus exalted Himself and His abilities above the Father in His own heart, He would have broken off His relationship of obedience and faith in the Father as a Son. As a result, Jesus would have haughtily turned His back on His Father's protection and provision. He ultimately would have stepped down from His heavenly position in the Father to lift Himself up in earthly prestige.

The illusion of worldly prominence based on achievements through self-striving may have lasted for some time, but He tragically would have lost heaven for the world. He would have chosen to embrace a worldly paradigm of living solely from Himself in an earthbound existence. As a result, He would eventually die in His own sin and be forever orphaned from His heavenly Father.

Conversely, Jesus lived by a heavenly paradigm. The apostle John stated that Jesus knew, "the Father had given all things into His hands, and that He had come from God and was going to God" (John 13:3 NKJV). Everything Jesus possessed was transmitted from the Father. In return, Jesus passionately determined to never take on a worldly way of life for all of the world to see that the Father was His source of life.

Jesus even told His disciples that when they looked at Him they were also looking at the Father (John 14:9). He perfectly collaborated with the Father without obstructing, in any way, the Father's radiant image shining through Him.

As a result of the Father's absolute love, provision, and care, Jesus trusted the Father would glorify Him in a far greater way than He would be able to exalt Himself in the world. Observe the following statements Jesus made regarding the transparent life of obedience and faith He had toward the Father:

"For I have come down from heaven, not to do My own will, but the will of Him who sent Me." (John 6:38 NKJV)

"He who speaks from himself seeks his own glory; but He who seeks the glory of the One who sent Him is true, and no unrighteousness is in Him." (John 7:18 NKJV)

"If I honor Myself, My honor is nothing. It is My Father who honors Me, of whom you say that He is your God." (John 8:54 NKJV)

The Bible clearly reveals that Jesus sacrificed the prospect of what He would do for His own personal gain, glory, and honor while living in the world.

In other words, Jesus remained a faithful Son, allowing the Father to shine through Him for all of the world to see the Father's heart toward humanity. Instead of selfishly striving to create His own independent life, He longed for the Father's love and life to be manifested through Him for the Father's gain and glory. Jesus eagerly collaborated with His Father to achieve the Father's love toward humanity on the Earth.

The Father's love led Jesus to the cross to accomplish the restoration of all things, including our relationship with the Father. In sacrificially honoring the Father, He knew that He was going to be restored to His rightful place in heaven after He died. He also understood that He was going back to His Father in a greater glory than what He was before He was sent into the world.

Glory of the Lamb

The only time Jesus had a self-oriented life, separate from the Father, was on the cross. The Bible says, "He made Him who knew no sin to be sin on our behalf, so that we might become the righteousness of God in Him" (2 Corinthians 5:21). The previous verse reveals that Jesus laid down His earthly life for the purpose of becoming our sinful nature, or old self, on the cross. He not only became sin in its root form, He also became our sinful person. He literally became the sinful, self-oriented enemy of God, and child of wrath that we were before believing in Him (Ephesians 2:3).

The moment He became sin on the cross, He was stricken with the wrath of God. He was separated from the Father for the first time in His eternal history. Jesus experienced the crucifixion of our old self-oriented life so that we can live a new righteous God-oriented life through Him.

The glory of the sacrificial Lamb was how He followed the Father straight to the death on the cross without wavering from His Father's will. Keep in mind that Jesus could have bowed down to satan by allowing His heart to focus on Himself instead of the Father. Satan tempted Jesus to live by a worldly paradigm of following His own life plan, creating His own person, making His own position in the world and taking His own possessions from the Earth apart from His heavenly Father.

Jesus did not follow the sinful course of the world by living such a vain and empty existence, devoid of the Father's purpose and plan for His life. On the other hand, Jesus boldly demonstrated to everyone that it was more rewarding to follow the Father's lead to a horrific death on the cross than to selfishly gain anything from the world.

Father's heavenly influence

The Father's heavenly influence defined who Jesus was and what He was sent to accomplish on Earth. Jesus had a heavenly identity, or profile, tailor-made for

Himself by His Father. The Father's profile for Jesus consisted of His Son's life plan, personhood, position and possessions from heaven. As long as Jesus remembered who He was and where He came from, the temptations of the world could never pull Him down from His heavenly position. Jesus perfectly fulfilled every characteristic of the heavenly profile to exemplify how a sent one from heaven does not become engrossed with a worldly profile.

The Father's heavenly influence also defined the life of Jesus with the cross. Look at how the Father used the crucifixion to express the ultimate portrayal of the Lamb's earthly life. The cross typified the sacrificial life Jesus lived out and later died to epitomize. The cross designated the position the Father chose for the Lamb in the world. The cross also defined what the Lamb would take from Earth into heaven, namely its marks on His body for a lasting memorial before the Father's throne.

Had Jesus lived to anything from the world before enduring the crucifixion, He would have been unworthy to offer Himself as an innocent and holy sacrifice. The Father's influence and heavenly profile helped Jesus remain focused on life above when He was tempted to turn to the sin of the world. The heavenly agenda of enduring the cross for the sins of humanity reminded Jesus of the earthly mission He was sent to accomplish. In the end, the cross graphically confirmed the reality that Jesus lived a sinless, blameless life before He was crucified.

Father's divine plan

Before Jesus was sent to Earth, He reigned in heaven alongside His Father with the view that the Father was more important than Himself. Jesus proved to all of creation in heaven and on Earth that the Father was more important than Himself by dying to accomplish the Father's redemptive plan for humanity. Jesus voluntarily paid with His blood to reconcile us to God as the propitiation for our sin (1 John 2:2).

Jesus virtuously paid with His ministry to make a way for us to fully live to God. Even as a boy, Jesus kept increasing in wisdom and stature (Luke 2:52). He continued learning His Father's ways and advancing in the kingdom of God through adulthood to show us how to fully live out a kingdom way of life. His maturity and ministry created a heavenly paradigm, profile, and pattern for us to follow in His "sent" ways on Earth.

The paradigm, profile, and pattern of Jesus is part of the Father's plan to bring us back to Himself before we die and go to heaven. When we participate in the paradigm, profile, and pattern of Jesus, we learn how to live to God as Jesus did. Therefore, Jesus was sent by the Father to create a heavenly paradigm, profile, and pattern to direct us to Himself.

We richly benefit from the heavenly paradigm and profile of Jesus as we walk out His divine pattern in our life. The divine pattern Jesus demonstrated during His life and ministry is as follows:

- Coming from heaven to manifest the Father's love.

- Orienting in the Father to live from heaven.

- Dying to self-oriented life through the cross.

- Experiencing resurrection life for the Father's glory.

- Reigning from heaven to enlarge the kingdom.

So far we have traced the life of Jesus up to the cross, which includes the first three points of His divine pattern listed above. The fourth point in the pattern of Jesus was clearly evidenced during the resurrection of Lazarus. Before Jesus resurrected Lazarus after being dead for days, He stated that He was the Resurrection and the Life (John 11:25). Jesus demonstrated the resurrection virtue He inwardly possessed by calling Lazarus out of the tomb. Subsequently, many believed in Jesus and glorified God when Lazarus shared his resurrection testimony.

Lastly, Jesus reigned from heaven through His position in His Father to fulfill the finished work of the cross. Remember, the work of the cross originated from the kingdom of heaven before the foundation of the world. Jesus aligned Himself to His Father in heaven in order to accomplish the work of the cross on Earth. In other words, Jesus lived out every point in His super-natural pattern to finish the Father's kingdom work up to and on the cross. Through Jesus, the kingdom of

God and a kingdom paradigm was established on Earth for all who choose to follow Him in His supernatural ways.

In the following contexts we will discuss the wisdom of God expressed through the supernatural paradigm, profile, and pattern of Jesus. The positional context explains how our old person was present in the Father's work of the cross in order for us to take part in His Son's supernatural pattern. Correspondingly, the experiential context explains how to live from the heavenly paradigm of Jesus and walk out His supernatural pattern as a sent one.

Collaborate with Jesus

The Father sent His Son to Earth to display the kind of relationship He wants with all of His children. Jesus said that He would not leave us as orphans (John 14:18). When we embrace Jesus as our life, He leads us into personal encounters with the Father's love and manifest presence. The Father's love brakes off anything deriving from being born into the world as a spiritual orphan. Furthermore, the Father's love empowers us to fully take on the life of sonship to completely embrace our identity and inheritance as His son or daughter.

Testimony

At this point, I wish to share a personal testimony of how my heavenly Father broke off the orphan spirit from my life. I will begin with some history of my past.

While growing up, I never had a close relationship with my earthly father due to the impositions of divorce and other factors that did not allow for us to spend much time together. I became a Christian at the age of twenty-two. Over time my passion for Jesus grew. Serving in the Church, mission trips, and telling people about Jesus was a passion of mine. I also loved God and the Holy Spirit, but focused on Jesus most of the time.

At the age of thirty-two I began attending a Messianic home group that allowed the Holy Spirit to move more freely than I had experienced in institutional and traditional Church settings. I was encouraged to move in the gifts of the Spirit, participated in deliverance ministry, and regularly preached before the small home group. I also became more acquainted with the Father and the kingdom during that time.

A few years later, Father sent me to another place of worship in order to understand His love toward me in a more intimate way. I went through a deliverance session with one of the Sozo ministry teams. The leader asked me to describe how I saw Father God. I replied by stating that I saw Him as a white mystery. My answer revealed how I mostly identified to Father as a distant God rather than an ever present father figure in my life. During the session, the Father was at work in my heart to break off restrictions that were hindering me from seeing and experiencing Him more closely.

One Sunday shortly after the session, He eventually broke through to me during a morning worship service. I must admit, this was an unsuspecting passion bomb dropped on me by my Dad in heaven.

The associate pastor called everyone forward to the front of the room for a more intimate time of worship. Before I could even settle in my space to worship, I fell to the floor next to one of the loud speakers. Father put His hand on me as I cried out in tears, yelling, "Why did you choose an orphan like me?" I did not ever think of myself as an orphan before that moment.

When I tearfully cried to my Abba in heaven, I understood more than ever before how much He loved me from before the foundation of the world (Ephesians 1:4). After worship time had ended, I rose to my feet knowing my Father more intimately and understood that He broke off an orphan spirit from my life during that personal encounter.

Encounter the Father

Perhaps you have not fully encountered your heavenly Father's love. I am talking about a powerful encounter from the Father that breaks off all hindrances from experiencing Him more fully; blockages such as an orphan spirit or religiosity. In my case, an orphan spirit, which is common even among Christians, prohibited me from intimately experiencing the Father's love.

In order for us to fully experience life with Jesus, we must engage the Father as Jesus did while He was on Earth. Jesus was not orphaned from the Father after being sent from heaven. He faithfully obeyed His Father as a loving Son within His Father's presence and care at all times.

Please pray the following prayer of adoption to become free of all restraints and fully experience Father's love as His child.

Prayer

Thank you Jesus, for not leaving me as an orphan. I choose to be adopted by my Father. I choose to have encounters with His powerful Fatherly love.

Father, my heart cries out to you for a spiritual adoption. Immerse me with the love that you had for me since before the foundation of the world. Through faith, I visit my home in heaven to experience your hugs and love. I also wait for your presence to manifest in my life on Earth.

Father! Break off all hindrances that keep me from your powerful love. I pray for the orphan spirit to be removed from my life. Replace the orphan mindset with its erroneous perception of who you are for an accurate picture of your loving nature. Also, wipe away the crippling thoughts and lies about the lack of your provision and care toward me. Cleanse my heart of deception that keeps me feeling lonely and unable to fit in as a vital part of your kingdom family.

I turn from religious affection and worldly deception that keeps me feeling as if I am always on the outside of your love, looking in for acceptance. By faith, I believe I am unconditionally loved and accepted in your heart because of your faithfulness toward me. Teach me how to celebrate who I am as a unique son/daughter for your good pleasure and my personal fulfillment.

Lastly Father, I choose to receive everything You place into my hands from heaven instead of striving to take up my own life in the world. I also choose to live out Your will on the Earth for Your glory, honor, and gain.

PART TWO:
POSITIONAL CONTEXT

"But God, who is rich in mercy, because of His great love with which He loved us, even when we were dead in trespasses, made us alive together with Christ (by grace you have been saved), and raised us up together, and made us sit together in the heavenly places in Christ Jesus." (Ephesians 2:4-6 NKJV)

The Bible contains verses that inform us on how we participated in Jesus' death, burial, resurrection and ascension to His throne in heaven. God made it possible for us to live out Jesus' supernatural pattern of being sent from heaven to Earth by having us participate in His historic crucifixion event.

We will first cover essential truth concerning the Holy Spirit and the kingdom message in order to understand the message of the cross more fully. Then, we will examine our participation in the work of the cross based on the Bible.

Holy Spirit

As discussed in the introduction, the Holy Spirit was with Jesus during His birth into the world. After Jesus was baptized by John the Baptist, John said, "I saw the Spirit descending from heaven like a dove, and He remained upon Him" (John 1:32 NKJV). The gentle Dove from heaven landed on the sacrificial Lamb. Likewise, we must be led by the Father as an obedient lamb before the heavenly Dove will land and remain on us.

The Apostle Luke stated that Jesus was full of the Holy Spirit after His baptism in the Jordan (Luke 4:1). Then, the Holy Spirit led Jesus to fast in the wilderness and directly face satan with his kingdom of darkness. Jesus returned victoriously from the place of satan's temptation in the power of the Spirit (Luke 4:14).

Jesus continued in His ministry doing all of the Father's works in the fullness and power of the Holy Spirit. Jesus even offered Himself up to the Father as a spotless sacrifice on the cross through the Holy Spirit (Hebrews 9:14). Following, the Holy Spirit raised Jesus from the dead to take the slain Lamb back to the Father (Romans 8:11).

The Holy Spirit also witnessed our participation in the death, burial and resurrection of the Lamb. The Apostle Paul, who sheds the most light on our participation in the death of Jesus, declared, "For to us God revealed them through the Spirit; for the Spirit searches all things, even the depths of God" (1 Corinthians 2:10). The Holy Spirit not only had a firsthand witness of the crucifixion, but He also searched out the full meaning of the cross within the Father's heart to understand its effects upon us.

Kingdom message

Father greatly glorified Jesus as the King of kings in His heavenly kingdom. For this reason, the Father gladly gave us the kingdom, because we are the kings and priests of His kingdom (Revelation 1:6). The kingdom of God defined in the Bible is righteousness, peace, and joy in the Holy Spirit (Romans 14:17). Jesus stated concerning the kingdom, "All things that the Father has are Mine. Therefore I said that He (the Spirit) will take of Mine and declare it to you" (John 16:15 NKJV). The Holy Spirit takes from what belongs to the King to establish the kingdom in our lives.

The Holy Spirit imparted an understanding of the kingdom message into Apostle Paul unlike anyone during his time. Apostle Paul stated, "the kingdom of God does not consist in words but in power" (1 Corinthians 4:20). He also stated, "Jesus is the power of God" (1 Corinthians 1:24). Likewise, Apostle Paul stated, "But of Him you are in Christ Jesus, who became for us wisdom from God" (1 Corinthians 1:30). Apostle

Paul gloried in his heavenly King while searching out the wisdom and power of the kingdom.

Regarding the kingdom message Apostle Paul stated:

"For since by man came death, by Man (the Son of Man) also came the resurrection of the dead. For as in Adam all die, even so in Christ all shall be made alive.

Then comes the end, when He (Lion of the Tribe of Judah) delivers the kingdom to God the Father, when He puts an end to all rule and all authority and power. For He must reign till He has put all enemies under His feet. The last enemy that will be destroyed is death.

Now when all things are made subject to Him, then the Son Himself (the Lamb) will also be subject to Him who put all things under Him, that God may be all in all." (1 Corinthians 15:21-22; 24-26;28 NKJV names of Jesus added for emphasis)

In the end, the Lion of the Tribe of Judah sacrificially presents the kingdom and Himself to the Father. The conquering Lion of the tribe of Judah lays down everything for the Father's glory just as He did before coming to Earth. At last, the heart of the Lamb is revealed within the triumphant Lion when He lays everything down for His Father.

Message of the cross

Apostle Paul wonderfully explained how God's kingdom rule was executed through the cross before all things were put under His feet. God wisely used the cross as an instrument of judgment where He "disarmed principalities and powers, He made a public spectacle of them, triumphing over them in it" (Colossians 2:15 NKJV). God triumphed over satan with his hierarchy of evil in the spiritual realm through the perfect sacrifice of His Son.

Although satan has been publicly defeated at the cross, he has not conceded to his downfall. He is still the god of this world (2 Corinthians 4:4). Satan continues to wage war on nations, families, and individuals with the intent of eternally separating people from God. His main determination is to steal, kill, and destroy through the structures of his dark kingdom established in the world (John 10:10).

Concerning the cross, Apostle Paul stated, "For the message of the cross is foolishness to those who are perishing, but to us who are being saved it is the power of God (1 Corinthians 1:18 & 23 NKJV). He also told the Galatians, "But God forbid that I should boast except in the cross of our Lord Jesus Christ, by whom the world has been crucified to me, and I to the world" (Galatians 6:14 NKJV). The truth contained in the message of the cross empowered Apostle Paul to overcome satan with his hierarchy of evil in the spiritual realm as well as his dark kingdom structures established in the world.

According to Apostle Paul, the message of the cross and the kingdom message were interrelated. One was not complete without the other. His cross to bear and the throne of the slain Lamb in heaven were not mutually exclusive.

Apostle Paul, who was an expert in the Jewish Law and a major contributor of the writings of the Christian faith, boldly stated to the Corinthians, "For I determined not to know anything among you except Jesus Christ and Him crucified" (1 Corinthians 2:2 NKJV). Why did Apostle Paul not say, "I determined not to know anything among you except Jesus Christ and Him enthroned in His heavenly kingdom?"

I am convinced Apostle Paul saw the crucified Christ first hand when he was translated to heaven (1 Corinthians 12:1-4). I believe Apostle Paul had an encounter with the crucified Christ in the center of the throne in heaven, much like the Apostle John in the book of Revelation. As a result, divine revelation of the cross, as it relates to the throne, poured forth from his heart through his writings.

In effect, Apostle Paul preached a message of the kingdom and the crucified King (1 Corinthians 1:23). Apostle Paul boldly declared that the kingdom would fully manifest in our lives as we completely identify with the crucified King of the kingdom.

Holy Spirit witness of the Lamb

When we receive Jesus into our hearts, we also receive the Holy Spirit into our newly created spirit. This is how our spirit is joined with the spirit of King Jesus (1 Corinthians 6:17). Apostle Paul also explained that, "we have received, not the spirit of the world, but the Spirit who is from God, that we might know the things that have been freely given to us by God"(1 Corinthians 2:12 NKJV). The Holy Spirit loves to give witness to the truth of the kingdom for our victory over the world.

Following, is the supernatural pattern of the Lamb as an outline to highlight significant Scripture verses that describe our participation in the crucifixion event. Supporting statements will express what the Holy Spirit witnessed concerning our seated place in heaven and the effects of the cross on our lives. Additional commentary is given to assist in assimilating the paradigm, profile, and supernatural pattern of Jesus as a central part of our own kingdom lifestyle.

Coming from heaven
to manifest the Father's love

The Holy Spirit is a witness to us being sent from heaven. Upon personally asking Jesus to become our King, our living spirit is sent from heaven to take up residence deep within us on Earth. Subsequently, we are miraculously transformed from being a spiritually dead human into a spiritually alive kingdom citizen (2 Corinthians 5:17).

As a kingdom citizen, we have the amazing privilege of carrying out a kingdom commission. Jesus prayed to the Father before enduring the cross, "As you sent Me into the world, I also have sent them into the world"

(John 17:18 NKJV). King Jesus authoritatively sent us from His heavenly throne into the world just as His Father sent Him.

We have been commissioned to do the Father's work just like the first disciples were after the resurrection of Jesus. He said, "Peace to you! As the Father has sent Me, I also send you (John 20:21 NKJV). Then He blew on them and told them to "receive the Holy Spirit" (John 20:22). Jesus blew the Holy Spirit on them to manifest the Father's love and life toward humanity.

Every believer succeeding the first disciples receives the same authority, power, jurisdiction and dominion to carry out the Father's heavenly commission through the Holy Spirit. When Jesus prayed to the Father to send His disciples from heaven He also prayed, "I do not pray for these alone, but also for those who will believe in Me through their word" (John 17:20 NKJV). Our response is to believe and know all of the kingdom rights and privileges that have been legally vested to us by the Father, paid in full through the sacrifice of Jesus.

By faith, we must take ownership of the kingdom commission that the Holy Spirit bears witness to in our spirit. We are legally entitled to all of the benefits of the kingdom through the sacrifice of Jesus. The Holy Spirit qualifies us, just as He did the first Apostles and early disciples, to exercise every right of the heavenly kingdom through the life of Jesus.

Obtaining everything that belongs to the kingdom begins with studying the life of Jesus from cover to cover in the Bible. Examine closely how Jesus was sent from heaven by the Father. We were sent from heaven with the authority, power, jurisdiction and dominion that He demonstrated on the Earth as the Son of Man. Jesus even said, "he who believes in Me, the works that I do he will do also; and greater works than these he will do, because I go to My Father" (John 14:12 NKJV). Jesus made the previous bold statement with us in mind.

Remember, Jesus paved the way for us to walk in His footsteps by taking on the form of a bondservant in the likeness of a man. How much more, now that Jesus has been resurrected as the glorified King of kings, does He desire to demonstrate His Kingly character, authority, and power through us to manifest the kingdom in all the Earth? This is why the author of the book of Hebrews instructed us to:

"Lay aside every weight, and the sin which so easily ensnares us, and let us run with endurance the race that is set before us, looking unto Jesus, the author and finisher of our faith, who for the joy that was set before Him endured the cross, despising the shame, and has sat down at the right hand of the throne of God." (Hebrews 12:1-2 NKJV)

Jesus despised the shame of the cross to demonstrate His glorious life through God's children on Earth.

Orienting in Jesus to live from heaven

The Holy Spirit is a witness to our position in heaven. When the Holy Spirit observes us, He perceives us from our seated place above in Jesus.

The Apostle Paul described the heavenly orientation every believer has in Jesus by stating,

"Therefore if you have been raised up with Christ, keep seeking the things above, where Christ is, seated at the right hand of God. Set your mind on the things above, not on the things that are on the earth. For you have died and your life is hidden with Christ in God. When Christ who is our life, is revealed, then you also will be revealed with Him in glory." (Colossians 3:1-4)

When we seek the things above, we align our heart and mind to spiritually rise above an earthbound orientation that is focused on self. We operate from our heavenly orientation with all of our heart, mind, will and emotions to discover who we really are in Jesus. As a result of passionately seeking Jesus, He responds with His manifest presence and glory in our lives so that we appear fully alive in Him before others.

With regard to our heavenly orientation and our position in Jesus, the Holy Spirit also keeps in mind our position in God's kingdom.

The Holy Spirit already knows who the governmental apostles, prophets, pastors, teachers and evangelists are for the equipping of the saints in the kingdom of God (Ephesians 4:11). Not everyone is in the foundational office of an apostle or a prophet (Ephesians 2:20), but due to the work of Jesus in our recreated spirit, every child of God has been made into His image as a saint.

We were spiritually recreated into a saint; therefore it cannot be earned by religious merit. We are saints that have been adopted into the family of God and make up the Church as the body of Christ (Ephesians 5:23). The kingdom of God is expressed through the previously mentioned five-fold governmental offices of the Church in collaboration with the ministry of the saints.

Some Christians dispute the idea of Jesus restoring the apostolic and prophetic offices in the Church. Still, it is necessary for every believer to understand that by virtue of their heavenly commission they are apostolic and prophetic saints within the kingdom of God.

Every believer has an apostolic and prophetic capacity within them, just as Jesus is within them. So, even if we have no desire to fill one of the offices in the Church government, we are called to be just as incredible and effective in our personal ministry as an apostolic/ prophetic saint (2 Timothy 4:5).

An apostle is a sent one. Jesus is described as the Chief Apostle and High Priest of our heavenly calling (Hebrews 3:1). Consider our heavenly commission in light of the Chief Apostle's paradigm, profile, and apostolic pattern. Our life is hidden in the Apostle above. We are sent from heaven to Earth through the Chief Apostle who transmits His love, life, authority and power into us to carry out the Father's apostolic mission for our life. As a result, we have the spiritual capacity and means to exercise our apostolic ability.

Concerning the prophetic, Apostle Paul stated, "Pursue love, and desire spiritual gifts, but especially that you may prophesy" (1 Corinthians 14:1 NKJV). As a follow up to his previous statement Apostle Paul also said, "For you can all prophesy one by one, so that all may learn and all may be exhorted" (1Corinthians 14:31 NKJV). According to Apostle Paul, no one is excluded from the practice of speaking life into another through the gift of prophecy.

Even Moses, under the Old Covenant, wished every Jew would prophecy and have God's Spirit upon them (Numbers 11:29). Moses also prophesied to them saying, "The Lord your God will raise up for you a Prophet like me from your midst, from your brethren. Him you shall hear" (Deuteronomy 18:15 NKJV). Yashua Ha Mashiac, the Hebrew name for Jesus Christ, is their Prophet and ours.

Now that we are in a new covenant with God through the blood of Jesus, we have a greater capacity to hear God's heart. Every believer who can hear God's heart and communicate His word in love has the ability to prophecy through the Prophet Jesus. Our commission from the Prophet qualifies us to prophecy as He chooses to speak through us wherever we are sent in His name.

Our life is literally from above, hidden in Jesus. Our life is hidden miles above the person we look at in the mirror. The more we orient our self in Jesus above, the clearer our view of our self comes into focus with how the Holy Spirit perceives us in our seated place.

Dying to self-oriented life through the cross

The Holy Spirit witnessed the crucifixion of our old self with Jesus on the cross. Satan thought God would have to forfeit all of humanity into his hands due to his legal right as the father of every sinful orphan since the fall of Adam and Eve (John 8:44). It is true that God abhorred how we were sinfully disobedient and wickedly corrupt to the core. We justly deserved nothing but condemnation and death for all of eternity.

However, the Father from heaven made a way for every orphan to be adopted into His family through the work of the cross. The Holy Spirit observed the death of our old self on the cross. He also witnessed the burial of our old person, entombed forever, out of the Father's sight.

Apostle Paul personally received the witness of the Holy Spirit concerning his death with Jesus on the cross. Apostle Paul celebrated being crucified with Christ by declaring, "I am crucified with Christ: nevertheless I live; yet not I, but Christ liveth in me: and the life which I now live in the flesh I live by the faith of the Son of God, who loved me, and gave Himself for me" (Galatians 2:20 King James Bible/Cambridge Ed.). Apostle Paul said that he was crucified with Christ. He undoubtedly personalized his participation in Jesus' death, burial, resurrection and ascension to heaven.

The practice of fully internalizing his new history of being crucified with Christ brought Apostle Paul into a greater experience with Jesus as his life. Eventually, his new history in Jesus had a greater influence on his new life than his own past from his old life. In a letter to the Philippians Apostle Paul recounted his past saying:

"For we are the true circumcision, who worship in the Spirit of God and glory in Christ Jesus and put no confidence in the flesh, although I myself might have confidence even in the flesh. If anyone else has a mind to put confidence in the flesh, I far more: circumcised the eighth day, of the nation of Israel, of the tribe of Benjamin, a Hebrew of the Hebrews; as to the law, a Pharisee; as to zeal, a persecutor of the church; as to the righteousness which is in the law, found blameless.

But whatever things were gain to me, those things I have counted as loss for the sake of Christ. More than that, I count all things to be loss in view of the surpassing value of knowing Christ Jesus my Lord, for whom I have suffered the loss of all things, and count them but rubbish so that I may gain Christ, and may be found in Him, not having a righteousness of my own derived from the law, but that which is through faith in Christ, the righteousness which comes from God on the basis of faith, that I may know Him and the power of His resurrection and the fellowship of His sufferings, being conformed to His death, in order that I may attain to the resurrection from the dead."
(Philippians 3:3-11)

The lengthy testimony from Apostle Paul points out his personal profile with an inventory of his past. Apostle Paul counted his religious position and all of his possessions as loss to gain Christ. It is clear that Apostle Paul released his own fleshly ambitions and plans to be laid hold of by Jesus.

Apostle Paul died to everything from his past that would hinder him from allowing Jesus to create his new spiritual profile of being a new person, taking on a new position, having new possessions and fulfilling his new destiny as a sent one from heaven.

We likewise need to personalize our participation in the death of Jesus to fully experience the benefits of our new history as a crucified child of God. Personally identifying with the crucifixion of the old person helps to differentiate the remnants of the old self within from who we really are in Jesus.

Likewise, understanding that our new history with Jesus has a greater impact on our lives than our old sinful past can set us free from the harmful consequences of the old life. Like Apostle Paul, we can die to our old self-made position, possessions, and plan to become transformed into the image of Jesus (2 Corinthians 3:18). The old life is sacrificed for the new to prove the perfect will of our Father.

Experiencing resurrection life
for the Father's glory

The Holy Spirit has witnessed the changes in our heart and behavior since becoming a believer in Jesus. Whether we completely understand it or not, deep inside, we cannot deny the burning passion to become transformed into the image of Jesus. We are also compelled to experience His resurrection life to accomplish supernatural works for the Father's glory.

Apostle Paul masterfully described how to be transformed into the image of Jesus and experience His resurrection life as our own stating:

"Therefore we have been buried with Him through baptism into death, so that as Christ was raised from the dead through the glory of the Father, so we too might walk in newness of life. For if we have become united with Him in the likeness of His death, certainly we shall also be in the likeness of His resurrection, knowing this, that our old self was crucified with Him, in order that our body of sin might be done away with, so that we would no longer be slaves to sin; for he who has died is freed from sin." (Romans 6:4-7)

Again, Apostle Paul personalized his new history with the burial of his old self. Then, he buried his past to walk by faith in newness of life.

In this instance though, Apostle Paul went beyond personalizing his new history in the death of Jesus. He ventured beyond believing what the Holy Spirit bore witness to in his spirit concerning his positional death in Jesus to experientially unite with Jesus' death and resurrection. Apostle Paul practiced the spiritual disciplines of Jesus that united him with the resurrection Lamb.

One such discipline was the practice of communion with Jesus through what is commonly called the Lord's Supper. He also prayed unceasingly, fasted regularly, engaged in spiritual warfare, and performed the supernatural works of Jesus among other disciplines mentioned in his writings. Apostle Paul clearly embraced the devotional disciplines as well as the demonstrative virtues of Jesus to express his newfound freedom in God.

Apostle Paul became alive to the sacrificial nature of the resurrected Lamb instead of remaining a slave to himself. He became united to the likeness of the resurrection life for the purpose of loving people, healing the sick, casting out demons, and raising the dead.

Like Apostle Paul, as a living sacrifice, we can become united in the death and resurrection of Jesus to do the supernatural works of the Father in newness of life.

Reigning from heaven to enlarge the kingdom

The Holy Spirit is a witness to Jesus reigning in heaven by the Father's side. All who belong to the King are able to reign with Him through the Holy Spirit. The Holy Spirit shows us how to obtain the rewards of the cross and the rights of the kingdom to invest the inheritance of the King in people (Colossians 1:12). For instance, we have been given every spiritual blessing in the heavenly places to give kingdom riches to others (Ephesians 1:3). By freely giving away the spiritual treasures of the King, both material and immaterial, we are in effect prevailing over the limitations of the world to spiritually benefit individuals.

The scripture clearly states that those who reign with Jesus are led by the Holy Spirit. Apostle Paul explained what it is like to reign through Jesus in this way:

"For all who are being led by the Spirit of God, these are the sons of God. For you have not received a spirit of slavery leading to fear again, but you have received a spirit of adoption as sons by which we cry out, "Abba! Father!" The Spirit Himself testifies with our spirit that we are children of God, and if children, heirs also, heirs of God and fellow heirs with Christ, if indeed we suffer with Him so that we may be glorified with Him." (Romans 8:14-17)

From the previous verses it is easy to conclude that reigning from heaven is a relational Father, Son, and Holy Spirit experience. Sons and daughters are no longer bound by a spirit of slavery and fear. As heirs, we carry on the kingdom legacy of the Father and Son through the Holy Spirit who testifies to our spirit. We cry out "Abba!" with all of our heart and carry the love of our Father wherever we go. Even if we inherit the sufferings of Jesus in this world, we will also be glorified with Him in the Father's kingdom.

We have been sent by King Jesus to fulfill the finished work of the cross and enlarge the kingdom of God on Earth. Jesus reigns in us as we exercise the work of the cross and the kingdom by the leading of the Holy Spirit.

Collaborate with Jesus

Jesus said He would not leave us alone in the world. He told His followers that He, "will ask the Father, and He will give you another Helper, that He may abide with you forever; that is the Spirit of truth, whom the world cannot receive, because it does not see Him nor know Him, but you know Him because He abides with you and will be in you" (John 14:16-17). Jesus said this to help us understand how to carry on His kingdom ministry after He rose from the dead to be with the Father in heaven.

During the earthly ministry of Jesus, the Holy Spirit worked with the disciples because of their association with Jesus. While the disciples were sent out by Jesus, the Holy Spirit went with them to heal the sick and cast out demons by virtue of their collaboration with Jesus. The Holy Spirit was among them but could not be in them because Jesus had not yet paid the price on the cross for their new life in Him.

After the resurrection, Jesus appeared before the disciples to hand over His kingdom ministry to them through a direct impartation of the Holy Spirit. Jesus breathed on them and told them to receive the Holy Spirit (John 20:22). They continued in the ministry with more love and power than they previously had in association with Him as a result of the impartation.

Unlike the early disciples who started doing supernatural works with Jesus through mere association, we begin our faith journey with His impartation of life inside of us. Upon asking Jesus to be our life, He breathes on our spirit. So, if we are powerless, we more than likely need an encounter with the Holy Spirit.

Encounter the Holy Spirit

The Holy Spirit is committed to confirm His witness of our positional participation in the paradigm, profile, and pattern of Jesus within every individual. Regularly studying the Bible prepares the heart to personally receive an impartation of truth and revelation directly from the Holy Spirit.

It is also necessary to have ongoing personal encounters with the Holy Spirit to experience the life of Jesus. Regular encounters with the Holy Spirit enables us to remain filled with the Spirit (Ephesians 5:18). Staying filled with the Spirit keeps us on fire for the things of the kingdom of God (Matthew 3:11). On top of that, being filled with the Spirit helps us grow in the fruit of the Spirit and exercise the gifts of the Spirit to do the works of Jesus in love (Galatians 5:22 and 1 Corinthians 12:8-11).

All of the aforementioned benefits, and much more listed in the Bible, is possible due to the work of the Holy Spirit through the process of sanctification. While it is gloriously true that Jesus is our sanctification (1 Corinthians 1:30), we also need the help of the Holy Spirit to become sanctified, or experientially set apart from the world (2 Thessalonians 2:13-14).

The Holy Spirit will lead us into all of the truth of Jesus as our life (John 16:13) including His heavenly paradigm, profile, and pattern. At the same time, He will direct us away from the former worldly paradigms, profiles, and patterns we were accustomed to following. We simply need to learn how to position ourselves to receive the sanctifying work of the Holy Spirit.

Eating the body and drinking the blood of Jesus on a daily basis is by far one of the best ways to allow the Holy Spirit to work on our behalf. Following is a personal testimony of the sanctifying work of the Holy Spirit through the Lord's Supper.

Testimony

I started practicing communion in my home around 2010. A book by Ana Méndez Ferrell named, *Eat my flesh, Drink my blood*, helped me understand that communion was never meant to be a religious act strictly confined within the walls of Church. Anna's stories of how her and her husband were supernaturally blessed during communion inspired me to believe for more while having fellowship with Jesus in my own home.

What I discovered is the Father, Son, and the Holy Spirit wanted to powerfully manifest their love and presence in my family's life.

First, I wish state that it took some time before the manifest presence of God broke out regularly during communion. Continue to be encouraged by the spiritual benefits of eating the body and drinking the blood of Jesus even though the Father's manifest presence may not break out right away. His spiritual light, life, and love feed our spirits so that we do not become spiritually deprived. We certainly do not neglect our physical bodies of food and drink. Why should it be any different for our spirits?

Secondly, we started out with wine and pita bread in the beginning and later found out that the Father loves to manifest strong in our lives even though crackers and water are used as the elements for the sacred meal. This may sound sacrilegious to some, but what matters most to our Father is the internal act of connecting our heart to His. Revering Jesus through communion on a daily basis captures our Father's heart. Following a religious script and adhering to external mechanics is simply not necessary in our own home.

We begin by straightforwardly asking Father, Jesus, and the Holy Spirit to manifest with their love and presence. Then, we authoritatively bind satan and demonic spirits that may be attacking our family. Afterward, the Holy Spirit usually leads us to experience communion in a different way than the time before.

Every communion is memorable for the unique experience each one offers.

Communion is the spiritually galvanizing experience that leads my family and I into loving God and each other more fully. The manifest love and presence of God excites us into pursuing every experience He has in store for us as a family and as unique individuals within His kingdom. The Holy Spirit has directed each of us to powerfully minister to each other. We have experienced physical healing, deliverance, inner healing, prophetic words, kingdom visions, baptism in the spirit, fire from heaven, anointing from the Lord and the glory of God first hand in our home. It is super-natural fun!

We have also seen the Holy Spirit powerfully minister to others through communion in their home. We have witnessed the presence of the Father, Jesus, and the Holy Spirit manifest in a similar way to what we have experienced in our own home.

Everything I am sharing with you and more is for all believers. Everyone that learns how to be led by the Holy Spirit will be directed into inviting Father's manifest presence in their home. Likewise, the Holy Spirit is passionate about leading us into uncommon kingdom experiences that connect us with Jesus more intimately through communion. Lastly, the kingdom experience in our homes enable us to minister more effectively wherever we are sent in the world.

The ongoing work of the Holy Spirit through communion helps us abide in the love of Jesus in ways that other spiritual activities do not afford. Please pray the prayer below to ask the Holy Spirit to work in your life in new ways. Also, prayerfully consider exercising your spiritual inheritance through communion by frequently partaking of the greatest riches within the kingdom of God, the body and blood of Jesus.

Prayer

Thank you Jesus for not leaving me on Earth without the Holy Spirit. I ask you to baptize me with the Holy Spirit and fire until there is a constant overflow of the Spirit into every area of my life. Burn away anything within me that does not belong to you Jesus! Keep me on fire in your Spirit and zeal.

Thank you Holy Spirit for your witness of my participation in the death, burial, resurrection and ascension to heaven. Teach me how to live out the supernatural pattern of being sent from heaven to Earth. I choose to live from a heavenly orientation in Jesus instead of solely from myself.

Teach me how to work with you in the process of sanctification. Show me when to die to the things that do not belong to Jesus and live to the things of God. Help me grow in your fruit and exercise your gifts to do the works of Jesus in love.

Lead me into the Father's heart and manifest presence. Show me how to live through the resurrection life of Jesus. Thank you!

PART THREE:
EXPERIENTIAL CONTEXT

"For Christ's love compels us, because we are convinced that one died for all, and therefore all died. And He died for all, that those who live should no longer live for themselves but for Him who died for them and was raised again." (2 Corinthians 5:14-15 NIV)

When Jesus followed the Father on Earth, He frequently talked about the cross and the kingdom of God. The Jews had heard their prophets proclaim the kingdom for hundreds of years before Jesus preached. As a result, many of them were expecting their long awaited Messiah to come and establish the kingdom on Israel's behalf.

During the time Jesus spoke about the cross, the Roman government occupied their God-given land. The Jews resisted being assimilated into the Roman customs and ways of life that were contrary to their own. They wholeheartedly believed their Messiah would deliver them from the oppressive presence of the Roman government.

Surely, the kingdom message of Jesus tugged on the hearts of most Jews. Many seriously weighed in on the possibility of Jesus being their long awaited Messiah. The message of the cross on the other hand, must have left many Jews in perplexity.

Most of the Jews knew the Roman government used a tall wooden cross as an instrument of death to cruelly punish wrongdoers. No doubt, the message of the cross was an offense to many of the Jews and a mystery to others.

Why would Jesus tell the Jewish people that they must take up a Roman cross? Following crowds were shocked by hearing incompatible statements about the anticipated kingdom of God and the repulsive Roman cross, such as:

"And he who does not take his cross and follow after Me is not worthy of Me." (Matthew 10:38 NKJV)

"If anyone wishes to come after Me, he must deny himself, and take up his cross and follow Me. For whoever loses his life for My sake and the gospel's will save it." (Mark 8:34-35)

"If anyone wishes to come after Me, he must deny himself, and take up his cross daily and follow Me." (Luke 9:23)

While the message of the cross was an enigma to just about everyone at that time, Father had a wise plan set in place since before the foundation of the world concerning its use. He used a Roman cross to enlist an army of Jesus collaborators that would enlarge His kingdom for generations after the crucifixion.

Yet, even though multitudes were enlisted to fight, only those who would die to themselves through the cross engaged in the battle. Unfortunately, many Christians throughout Church history did not stop living for themselves because they did not see that they were crucified with Jesus on the cross.

Seeing the cross in Jesus

The meaning of the cross has been hidden from the world even though its symbolism has endured over the centuries. Its message is a mystery to many today as it was when Jesus spoke about it long ago.

People do not perceive the freedom and beauty of the cross because there is only one possible way of seeing its multifaceted wisdom. Clear revelation of the cross comes directly from the one who wholeheartedly embraced it in His life, even before enduring the crucifixion in our place.

Evidence of the work of the cross is seen within the life of Jesus when the devil tempts Him. Satan often pushed his schemes before Jesus to turn Him away from His Father. Most notably, he offered Jesus a spectacular vision of prestige and power in a worldly kingdom. All the kingdoms of the world and their glory were offered to Jesus if He would bow down and worship satan (Matthew 4:8).

The worldly vision presented a high position and vast array of possessions to Jesus if He followed satan's plan for His life. In that moment of decision, Jesus experienced a clash of visions. Jesus was faced with the choice of following His Father's vision of the heavenly kingdom within Him or the vision of satan's kingdom in the world. Satan attempted to lure Jesus with the glory of a worldly kingdom for the purpose of blinding Him to the inner vision of the kingdom of God.

Jesus compared His Father's vision within His heart to the one satan projected before His mind. In contrast, He saw a glory in His cross that satan could not easily imitate. With the cross in view, He was able to exercise wise spiritual judgment and remain faithful to His Father. He decided to take up the high virtue of self-denial for the purpose of glorifying God instead of Himself. Then, He laid down His life in the essence and expression of the cross to deny the self-exaltation inherent in satan's lies.

Judgment of the cross

Unfortunately, all matters of life are not easily seen as black or white issues. One must spiritually judge to discern right from wrong and truth from lies. Therefore, spiritual judgment is required to remain in God's light at all times.

The reality of spiritual complexities necessitates a full comprehension of the cross to both accurately see and rightly judge spiritual anomalies in the world. This is especially true when it comes to the glory of the world and the counterfeit light of satan (2 Corinthians 11:14). Otherwise, even long standing believers may be deceived into following the ways of the world instead of promoting the kingdom of God.

Spiritual judgment is the ability to make the best decisions to remain in God's perfect will for our life. Although one aspect of the judgment of the cross has to do with wrath against sinfulness, another encompasses the ability to make the most excellent conclusions for our life.

Jesus addressed the topic of judgment by stating, "For judgment I came into the world, so that those who do not see may see, and that those who see may become blind" (John 9:39). Jesus came into the world to open the spiritual eyes of the spiritually blind. Conversely, those who think they see on their own are blind to the life of Jesus. According to Jesus, judgment includes the ability to spiritually see our life in Him.

He also pointed out what righteous judgment was when questioned on His controversial practice of healing during the Sabbath. Accusatory and critical observers of the Law of Moses were answered with the following:

"If a man receives circumcision on the Sabbath so that the Law of Moses will not be broken, are you angry with Me because I made an entire man well on the Sabbath?

Do not judge according to appearance, but judge with righteous judgment." (John 7:23-24)

Notice above that Jesus did not defensively tell the religious leaders who questioned His actions to stop judging Him. Why? To do so would grossly misrepresent the Father.

Remember, God is a collaborator. Father was interested in more than telling the critics what to think through the Law. Likewise, He was focused on more than telling them how to think through religion. He was much more concerned with teaching them how to think for themselves by following the example of Jesus. In doing so, they would break out of the religious mindset that prevented them from accurately perceiving the motive of Jesus. Then, they could work with God in righteous judgment to heal others and fulfill the law of love just like Jesus.

Father directed Jesus to heal on the Sabbath to confront the religious views of the day. According to the religious leaders, the ministry of healing was considered work that God forbade the Jews to do on the Sabbath (Exodus 20:10). The religious authorities overlooked the purpose of the Law, which was to make men whole and restored back to God. They judged according to the outward appearance of work on the Sabbath. They concluded that Jesus had violated the Law when He actually fulfilled it. Ironically, the religious men who claimed to know the will of God could not be any further from the heart of the Father in their un-righteous judgment.

Judgment of the cross, in respect with spiritually seeing, is strengthened by taking up our cross daily. It gives us discernment to distinguish the new life from the old life we were once enslaved to in the world. Spiritual judgment shows us how to think for ourselves by denying old mindsets to hear the heart of our Father. It empowers us to defy what we were told to think by man to work with God. Lastly, righteous judgment guides us to follow the example of Jesus and fulfill the law of love.

Seeing the kingdom within

As we learn how to clearly see our life in Jesus, it becomes easier to focus on our God-given kingdom vision. A kingdom vision is the bigger picture of how our life through Jesus makes an impact in the world for the kingdom of God.

Vision casting was an impressionable vehicle both sides of the battle used in the fight for the heart of Jesus. It is no different for us today. Father, Jesus, and the Holy Spirit work in perfect harmony to give divine revelation of a personalized plan and a kingdom vision for every believer to live out. Jesus is the collaborative visionary for our life. The Holy Spirit leads us into the fullness of our life story, vision, destiny and personalized plan of God for our life.

Satan, on the other hand, knows the glory of the worldly kingdom is deceptively attractive to those who cannot spiritually see the kingdom of God. He understands people will eventually take ownership of an alluring worldly vision if they do not discover a God-given vision of their own.

Think of a kingdom vision as God's creative way of capturing our heart and mind so that we will no longer desire to live for ourselves. The more we grow in our capacity to spiritually see, discern, and judge the kingdom within, the greater our imagination and faith is empowered to push the creative limits of living through Jesus. With increased spiritual sight and judgment, our vision is enlarged within our hearts, enabling us to see how life with Jesus grants more freedom of personal expression than life apart from God.

Sent paradigm of Jesus

Jesus demonstrated a paradigm for us to live by from above. The world presents many to live by on the Earth. The paradigm we personally choose, heavenly or worldly, profoundly influences our life within and without. So, what is a paradigm?

As mentioned previously, satan tempted Jesus with all the kingdoms of the world. It appeared as though satan was offering Jesus a high position of rulership and privilege within a glorious worldly kingdom. Imagine the position, possessions, and plan satan was promising Jesus. Even still, think of the kind of person Jesus would have become in satan's kingdom.

Satan's real intent was to deceive Jesus into living by a worldly paradigm, not becoming a ruler over the worldly kingdom. Ironically, a worldly paradigm would have subjugated Jesus under satan's rule. The glory of the world would influence Jesus to live from an earth-bound orientation, directing His heart to worship satan and the things of the world. Consequently, He would live by a worldly paradigm of self-exaltation and striving for illegitimate gain as a slave to satan.

Jesus alluded to the worldly paradigm several times in the gospels. For example, He stated, "For what will it profit a man if he gains the whole world and forfeits his soul" (Matthew 16:26). In another passage He stated, "He who has found his life (soul) will lose it, and he who has lost his life for my sake will find it" (Matthew 10:39 NASB). Jesus was sharing an opportunity for the crowds to reject the worldly life for a new kingdom life found only in Him.

The Bible highlights major categories of worldly paradigms. Some of which are the paradigms of self, sin, and religiosity. Each category is an eye opening study in itself. Below is a list of Bible verse references containing some of the most common paradigm comparisons.

Paradigm comparison by Jesus (Matthew 10:38)
- Sent paradigm- Take up cross/Worthy of Jesus.
- Former Paradigm- Loves family, Church, and the world more than Jesus.

Paradigm comparison by Jesus (Matthew 16:24)
- Sent paradigm- Take up cross/Deny self to gain Jesus
- Former Paradigm- Follow self to gain the world

Paradigm comparison by Jesus (Mark 8:34)
- Sent paradigm- Take up cross/Deny self for the gospel (good news about Jesus)
- Former Paradigm- Follow self-glorifying message or selfish life story

Paradigm comparison by Jesus (Luke 9:23)
- Sent paradigm- Take up cross/Die daily to live to God
- Former Paradigm- Live to self/Die to who you are and what you have in Jesus

Paradigm comparison by Jesus (Luke 14:27)
- Sent paradigm- Take up cross/Be a disciple and fulfill personal God-given destiny
- Former Paradigm- Abort God-given destiny by following a family plan and/or self-centered plan

Paradigm comparison by Apostle Paul (Galatians 6:14)
- Sent paradigm- Die to the world/Crucified to the world
- Former Paradigm- Alive to the world and the world's ways

Paradigm comparison by Apostle Paul (Galatians 2:20)

- Sent paradigm- Die to self/I no longer live apart from the life of Jesus
- Former Paradigm- Live to self apart from the faith of Jesus

Paradigm comparison by Apostle Paul (Galatians 5:23)

- Sent paradigm- Die to the flesh/Crucified sinful passions and selfish desires
- Former Paradigm- Slave to the flesh, passions, and etc.

Paradigm comparison by Apostle Paul (Galatians 2:19)

- Sent paradigm- Die to the law/Live to God
- Former Paradigm- Live to the law and religiosity

Paradigm comparison by Apostle Peter (1 Peter 2:24)

- Sent paradigm- Die to sin/Live to righteousness
- Former Paradigm- Live to sin and unrighteousness

A simple definition of a paradigm is an example, pattern, template, standard or model. Think of a paradigm as an example that offers a possible framework of much needed solutions for life. The earthly example of Jesus is our solution to every challenge of living as a sent one from heaven.

Jesus "knew" His paradigm of choice. Since He lived from above, He understood the perspective of life from above. He purposely refused to live by the worldly paradigms because He was not of the world. He chose a paradigm that offered a kingdom view of seeing from above. The sent paradigm offered Jesus a higher perspective for answers to the challenges of living on Earth as a sent one from above.

The paradigmatic verse, John 13:3, is a key that unlocks what the sent paradigm meant to Jesus. The apostle John stated that Jesus knew "the Father had given all things into His hands, and that He had come from God and was going to God" (John 13:3 NKJV). Jesus believed the Father had given all things into His hands. Jesus took comfort in knowing Father God unconditionally loved Him. He also took confidence in how Father God unconditionally invested all things into His hands. Father God absolutely, unreservedly, fully and freely invested Himself for Jesus to succeed in accomplishing His will on Earth. The heavenly paradigm provided spiritual and kingdom resources for life on Earth.

Lastly, He knew where He had come from and where He was going. Jesus was sent to Earth while keeping His occupancy in heaven above. For Jesus, living sent from above meant allowing His position in His Father to have a greater influence in His life than His own existence on Earth. The heavenly paradigm gave Jesus the orientation and direction He needed to remain focused and faithful to the high calling on His life until He would be reunited with His Father again.

The sent paradigm of Jesus casts a vision of living as a sent one from above. A sent vision is the capacity of spiritually seeing how we were sent into the world just as Jesus was sent into the world by His Father. Like Jesus, we were sent from heaven, have been given all things into our hands by our Father, and will be going back to our Father in heaven. We prepare our heart and mind to receive the sent vision by personalizing the sent paradigm, profile, and pattern of Jesus on a daily basis. As our life becomes redefined within the sent paradigm, profile, and pattern of Jesus, we mature in His experiential context to collaborate with Him.

Sent profile of Jesus

Our lives are constantly challenged with the impulse to create our own person, position, plan and amassing our own possessions in this world apart from the Father's leading. Such is the result of inheriting a worldly paradigm of self-seeking for personal gain. The worldly way of life has been embedded deeply into our soul, dramatically defining our mind, will, and emotions within a worldly context. Unbeknownst to us, our lives have been re-strained within the limitations of a worldly paradigm that naturally integrated us into a stifling worldly profile and pattern of living.

The sent profile of Jesus is fundamentally different than that of the world. Jesus was sent into the world to reveal the Father in all of His love and glory toward humanity. The Father had to be seen within and expressed through Jesus for the Father to be glorified on the Earth. Therefore, the Father designed the sent profile to express Himself through Jesus from the inside out.

Jesus knew He was sent as the Son of God, the Father had a plan for His life, the cross was His position in the world and His possessions were from the kingdom of heaven. His Father was never left out of the equation of life. Jesus understood that creative collaboration had to be the impetus of His sent profile to remain true to His Father and Himself.

Since our life is hidden in Jesus, our new profile is found in Him as well. Living as a sent one from heaven is remarkably different than living solely from ourselves on Earth.

As a result, factoring in our plan, person, position and possessions from above requires constant readjustment within ourselves. This is due to what was assimilated into our life while living in the world apart from God.

A personal revelation of being crucified with Jesus greatly speeds up the process of purging the world out of our life. Jesus died on the cross to develop in us the capacity and ability to spiritually die to the former plan, person, position and possessions of the worldly life.

Presenting ourselves alive to God as Jesus authors our life plan, creates our person in Him, sets our position in the kingdom and gives us our possessions from heaven is what the sent profile is all about (Romans 6:13). In doing so, there is substantially more to create with when we place our life in the hands of Jesus. What we obtain for ourselves using our own hands is nothing compared to what Jesus offers, even if we selfishly gain the whole world.

The sent profile is consistent with the supernatural kingdom of heaven, whereas the worldly profile mainly consists of things that are relegated to the natural elements of the world. One gives a high calling to operate in creative collaboration with the creator of heaven and Earth. The other suggests a compromised life of selfishly following the ways of the world.

Personalizing the sent profile

The sent profile aligns believers to their life in Jesus. Consistently personalizing the sent profile reinforces a personal identity of being a sent one from heaven.

The next two pages contain a brief worldly and sent profile list. Fill in all of the personal information necessary for seeing the old and new life in both profiles. Use the *Collaborate Move•Meant* guide as an aid for your answers.

The information collected from the profile comparison will provide strong clues into the kind of kingdom vision the Father has for us. Do not be quick to disregard past aspects of life in the worldly profile. Jesus may redeem elements from the old life to be used for the Father's glory in the future.

Regular review of the sent profile will help us grow in our identity and destiny in Jesus. Share findings with at least one confidant. The feedback and accountability will be a necessary support for the most challenging growth areas of life.

My old worldly profile

- My self-made plan for life apart from God

- Type of person I desired to be apart from God

- Position(s) I strove for in the world

- Possessions I desired for myself

- Sinful path I followed in the world

Concluding statement about the self-oriented life of living to sin and dying to the Father, Jesus, and the Holy Spirit.

My new sent profile

- Father's plan for my life

- Type of person Father created me to be

- Position the Father set for me in the kingdom

- Possessions given to me from the Father

- Kingdom path I am called to lead

Concluding statement about the collaborative life I experience with the Father, Jesus, and the Holy Spirit.

Sent pattern of Jesus

The sent pattern Jesus demonstrated during His earthly ministry is ours to experience through His life. Jesus has written our life story within His sent paradigm, profile, and pattern to make a way for us to supernaturally collaborate with Him on Earth.

We will review the sent pattern as an outline for an experiential perspective of following Jesus. Relational concepts are presented in a type of cause and effect scenario to enhance our relationship with the Father, Jesus, and the Holy Spirit. In conjunction, visionary ideas systematically develop a strong case for what it means to collaborate with Jesus as a sent one.

Coming from heaven to manifest the Father's love

Coming from heaven to manifest the Father's love can be simplified into a two-part process, aligning and applying ourselves to God's will. We must align ourselves to the Father's heart in preparation to apply ourselves to His will. The disciplines of aligning and applying ourselves is more of an art form than a science, particularly with acts of love and the supernatural works of Jesus.

The practice of aligning ourselves involves getting our heart into the best position to the Father's heart. By virtue of our deep love for the Father, the simple act of inviting His presence by calling on His name out loud may be enough to align our heart to His. At other times, we discover the need for a higher virtue to connect with the Father, which is not always easily found within ourselves.

Depending on the condition of our heart at the time, or the circumstances we may be in, there are moments we find it impossible to align ourselves to the Father without His direct intervention. Apostle Paul's encouragement for such moments of inner conflict is to, "work out your salvation with fear and trembling; for it is God who is at work in you, both to will and to work for His good pleasure" (Philippians 2:12-13). God is the originator of the high virtue we need within ourselves to keep us intimately connected to His heart.

The Father is at work inside of us to bring us higher into His heart in ways we can not do so on our own. His higher virtue enables us to align our will with His to rise above the lower virtues of life that are of no help in fully pursuing Him. When we align with His heart, we can come to Him or commune with Him in our spirit. His love compels us to apply ourselves to the works of Jesus for His good pleasure. Intimacy with our Father moves us to share His love and life with all who do not know His heart.

One of the strongest ways the Father urges us to wholeheartedly commit to His higher virtue is by birthing a kingdom cause within our heart. A cause is defined as a principle, aim, or movement that, because of a deep commitment, one is prepared to defend or advocate (*New Oxford American Dictionary*). Father's deep work in us prepares our hearts to participate in His *Collaborate Move•Meant* by personally taking up a kingdom cause.

Whatever the kingdom cause, be convinced of this, it will be worth giving our life for even though it may not be fulfilled within our lifetime.

A cause that is birthed by our Father comes from heaven. The purpose for a heavenly cause is to manifest the Father's love and life through a form of kingdom advocacy in the world. An advocate is a person who publicly supports individuals, or group of people, who are unable to help themselves in some crucial way. The Father is determined to fully develop who we are as a kingdom advocate. He is at work to birth a well defined kingdom cause within us to meet the critical needs of others.

Defined kingdom cause

The Father's high virtue is at work within us to clearly define a kingdom cause for our life. A strong kingdom cause is largely defined by foundational and central truths that give way to its inception. The Father defines the foundational truths we are to stand on to boldly stand up for our cause. He also shows us the central truths we revolve our life around to propel our cause with greater momentum.

There are corporate foundational and central truths the body of Christ builds on to remain centered in the Father's will as a Church. Effective advocacy of the local Church carries out the Father's heart toward surrounding communities.

Participants personally benefit from supporting the advocacy efforts of the Church. Church advocacy is a great opportunity to undergo formal training towards a personal kingdom enterprise. Selflessly committed advocates that know how to apply their formal training are empowered to embark on a personal kingdom undertaking of their own.

The Father is interested in a personal enterprise for every believer, just as He is with corporate advocacy through the Church. Unfortunately, many Churches do not usually train believers in the disciplines of forging a personal God-given cause or kingdom undertaking. As a result, many people are not encouraged to fully step into their unique personal calling. Unless individuals have a strong sense of destiny for their life, an undiscovered or underdeveloped kingdom cause will lay dormant within them as a result.

Thankfully, the Father is growing us up and maturing us to stand out as unique individuals among the body. One obvious reason for this is to express His infinite creativity through a specialized calling for every individual. Another reason has to do with a multiplication of advocacy efforts to exponentially enlarge His kingdom around the world. The Father chose to diversify advocacy and kingdom enterprise through a variety of individualized causes to reach every type of person on Earth.

Lastly, the Father will direct us to work out our salvation to live from heaven because His kingdom is within us who believe (Luke 17:21). A personal vision, mission, and core values are creative disciplines that help us to discover the kind of individualized life the Father dreamt for us. These creative measures also work to bring out the kingdom from within us into the world. They help us focus on unique strengths that are necessary to express the kingdom in ways we were individually designed to affect the world. A kingdom vision, mission, and values aid in working out our personal salvation as they help us become more of who we were authentically created to be in Jesus. Experiential salvation takes place when we cease participating in our old life to advance in our new personal vision, mission, and values through Jesus.

Orienting in Jesus to live from heaven

During the heavenly orientation process, it is necessary to allow our earthly, old life to pass away. Apostle Paul emphasized the contrast between our old and new life stating, "Therefore if anyone is in Christ, he is a new creature; the old things passed away; behold, new things have come" (2 Corinthians 5:17). We must firmly believe in our hearts with a fierce faith in Jesus that there is no longer anything worth holding onto in our old life.

Our faith in action is the powerful expression of our true person hidden in Jesus. Through faith, the old person fades away while our new person shines brighter and brighter. By faith, we are poised to overcome all personal shortcomings and every self-created adversity of the old life.

The Bible defines faith as the substance of things hoped for, the evidence of things not seen (Hebrews 11:1 NKJV). The writer of Hebrews also had the following definitive statement to say about faith, "without faith it is impossible to please Him, for he who comes to God must believe that He is, and that He is a rewarder of those who diligently seek Him (Hebrews 11:6). Faith is one of the strongest spiritual dynamics that lead us upward to our Father in heaven.

An increasing love for the Father and growing faith in Jesus will stir our soul to live from above at all times. We will want to adjust our life and orient ourselves in our position in Jesus to constantly commune with the Father. Our desire will be for nothing less than the Father's manifest love and presence.

As we become oriented to our seated place in Jesus, we learn how to operate from His heart and mind. Our heart becomes more like His heart. Our mind becomes transformed to think like His mind thinks (Romans 12:2 and 1 Corinthians 2:16). We also grow in Christ consciousness, which is the state of being awake and aware of our life in the heavenly places in Him. Christ consciousness from an earthly perspective is being awake and aware of Jesus as our life when we move and have our being through Him.

Authentic Christ consciousness is not to be confused with the universally accepted type of "Christ consciousness" that purportedly brings about a heightened spiritual enlightenment, further empowering humankind to evolve into godhood through human effort. True Christ consciousness, on the other hand, brings us into a complete understanding of how Jesus is God, and we are not. As we grow in Christ consciousness, we become acutely aware of how the Father raised us up out of the depths of depravity into a heavenly position we could never attain on our own. We also awaken to the truth that apart from the life of Jesus we can do nothing of kingdom value (John 15:5). This is why Jesus said, "it is enough for the disciple that he become like his teacher, and the slave like his master" (Matthew 10:25). Christ consciousness empowers us to experience intimate oneness with Jesus to become more like Him. Surrendering to Jesus to put on His consciousness is far more fulfilling than walking in a delusion of grandeur, thinking that we are a god on the Earth.

In addition, the worldly adaptation of Christ consciousness does not acknowledge that Jesus is the only way to enter a relationship with God. On the contrary, Jesus said, "I am the way, and the truth, and the life; no one comes to the Father but through Me" (John 14:6). Jesus also claims to be the only way in which anyone can enter the kingdom of God, stating, "I am the door; if anyone enters through Me, he will be saved, and will go in and out and find pasture" (John 10:9). After we become saved through Jesus, we are free in Him to explore the kingdom, finding rest from the old life and worldly paradigms.

A higher morality

Christ consciousness leads to new, higher morals. A definition for morals is a person's standards of behavior or beliefs concerning what is and is not acceptable for them to do (*New Oxford American Dictionary*). A consistent spiritual orientation in Jesus makes us aware of His standards for beliefs and behavior concerning what is and is not acceptable for a believer.

More specifically, Jesus imparts His moral virtue into our lives so that we can live up to His higher standards of living. Impartation is a supernatural download of His life into ours for the purpose of empowering us to live like Him. The supernatural impartation of His morals into our life gives us higher "supermorals" for a new supermoral lifestyle.

A supermoral lifestyle is the result of believing the higher morals of Jesus are ours as well because of His life within us. The life of Jesus in us holds us to the high standard of living on Earth as He lived. His life in our spirit gives us the innate ability to prophecy, heal the sick, and cast out demons just as He did while on Earth. The previously mentioned abilities of Jesus become our new core capabilities that exhibit our supermoral lifestyle.

The belief that supernatural life is for every believer is a fundamental moral of the kingdom of God. As a result, incorporating the supernatural life of Jesus into everyday circumstances becomes our new moral obligation. We no longer save our life for ourselves by keeping the life of Jesus inside of us from others. We freely give our supernatural love and life away to benefit people. Holding back love, healing, and deliverance from individuals when the life of Jesus in us can set them free is no longer acceptable.

When we exercise our faith in Jesus, we learn how to supermorally conduct ourselves to supernaturally benefit others. As a result, Jesus will enable us to empower others in ways we could never accomplish on our own.

Dying to self-centered life through the cross

Dying to ourselves is not an option while living on Earth. We will die to ourselves in one of the two following ways. Apostle Paul brilliantly explained how death to ourself is unavoidable saying, "if you are living according to the flesh, you must die; but if by the Spirit you are putting to death the deeds of the body, you will live (Romans 8:13). Option one of living according to the flesh leads to spiritual and physical death. Option two leads to life if we put to death the sinful deeds of the flesh through the work of the Holy Spirit.

According to the previous verse, we can die to our true self by living in the flesh. The flesh is the expression of our old life apart from God. It is the expression of who we were before Jesus made us who we really are in Him. The flesh entertains the thoughts of our old self and carries out the conduct of our old life. It literally wages war against our soul. It will never surrender until it is manifested on the outside of us to the point of conforming us to the world.

Although our spirit is made alive in Jesus, our mind, will, and emotions conform to the old life when we allow the flesh to override our love for Jesus. Consequently, our true self remains suppressed within us when we give ourselves over to the flesh. Therefore, crucifying the flesh to death on a daily basis is the only way of overcoming it.

Unfortunately, the flesh does not only operate when we willfully do what God does not want us to do, or when we deliberately walk in sin. The flesh can also drive us into sin when we do outwardly "good" things. This is possible because the flesh also wages war with the Holy Spirit inside of us (Galatians 5:17). The flesh strives to replace the guiding presence of the Holy Spirit over our life. Unless our actions are led by the Holy Spirit, they will be motivated by the flesh. The deeds of the body must be put to death so that we are led by the Holy Spirit with pure motives.

In the same way, we must die to self-centered life to truly live. Jesus repeatedly told us to deny the old self, take up our cross, and follow Him. At the point of self-denial, self-centeredness ceases to be the driving force of our life.

Denying our self is instinctually one of the most uncharacteristic measures we consider taking for ourselves. It is only natural to be concerned about the cost of losing something of value that we have invested in over time. Often times, the loss is associated with extreme pain.

Unfortunately, the immediate price of pain can inhibit our ability to sacrifice for a proportionately greater reward.

One of the creative ways Jesus motivates us to deny ourself is by placing conviction in our heart. Conviction is a strongly held belief. When we sell out to Jesus, we are willing to die to ourselves to champion our conviction in the world.

A commonly held belief may require lifestyle changes to fully own up to the truth it contains. Conviction drives us to take radical measures in demonstrating the truth our strongly held beliefs convey in our heart.

Our conviction translates through our behavior to the degree that we are convinced of our strongly held beliefs. For example, many people have heard and believe that Jesus is returning again very soon. When someone is fully convinced His return will be within a few years, they will behave accordingly. If another believes in their head the fact that Jesus is coming again soon, but is not convinced in their heart to the point of self-denial, life will carry on as usual without any lifestyle change.

Supernatural ability to do nothing

Our conviction to collaborate with Jesus is as strong as the extent we are convinced He wants to be our life. Remember, collaboration with Jesus involves dying to ourself as well as living to Him. Jesus offers His life to make it possible to die to ourself, sin, the world, religiosity and the influence of our spiritual enemies.

The truth is, we cannot die to self-centered life without His life in us. This is to His glory.

Before we entered into a relationship with Jesus, we existed in the world with the inability to die to sin. Now that we are one with Jesus, He gives us the supernatural ability to do nothing. Yes, it possible to be supernatural while doing nothing in the world. It is a supernatural feat to have nothing to do with self-centered life, sin, the world, religiosity and our spiritual enemies. Not living to the aforementioned spectrum of worldly paradigms and dark kingdom structures is evidence of being supernaturally alive to Jesus.

Our ability to supernaturally do nothing is possible through the self-denying virtue of Jesus. When we learn how to thrive in His high virtue of self-denial we will become a living sacrifice. As a living sacrifice, with uncommon conviction, we will lay everything down to accomplish our kingdom cause through Jesus.

Experiencing resurrection life for the Father's glory

Dead people are perfect candidates for resurrection life. This is simply what the cross of every believer is all about. Crucifying the old life is more about positioning ourselves for the resurrection life of Jesus than it is with placing our old man on the cross. The cross is meant to be a reminder of the resurrection virtue of Jesus within the crucified believer. The beauty of His resurrection virtue is the way it reaches down far to pull us up out of the depths of death.

The Resurrection Himself is our life. His resurrection life in us is the resurrection standard for us. His determination through His resurrection virtue is to raise us up out of the old life of immorality and status quo standards for living. In this particular case, resurrection virtue directly relates to the moral virtue of Jesus within the believer.

Resurrection virtue is also the resurrection power of Jesus. Apostle Paul addressed the resurrection power within every believer by stating, "the Spirit of Him who raised Jesus from the dead dwells in you, He who raised Christ Jesus from the dead will also give life to your mortal bodies through His Spirit who dwells in you" (Romans 8:11). We have access to the resurrection power of Jesus through the Holy Spirit inside of us.

Jesus defied the natural limitations of this life by doing creative miracles, signs, wonders, and raising the dead. He exercised creative conventions that destroyed sickness, disease, and death. His kingdom way of life established a new norm that did not blindly accept the natural consequences of life without question. The supernatural creative conventions of Jesus make it possible to overcome the ailments of life in uncommon ways.

As we experience the resurrection virtue of Jesus, an increasing desire to apply ourselves to His creative conventions develops in our heart. Faith in Jesus directs us to release His resurrection virtue into the lives of others. Our core competencies of prophesying, healing the sick, and casting out demons strengthen. The creative conventions of doing miracles, signs, and wonders become part of our lifestyle.

Now that Jesus is in heaven, He has personally delegated His supernatural ministry to us through His great commission. Our King told us to go into all of the world and teach everyone to observe all of His commands (Matthew 28:20). He also commanded us to go and preach saying, "the kingdom of heaven is at hand (Matthew 10:7). Then He told us to demonstrate the kingdom by healing the sick, raising the dead, cleansing the lepers and casting out demons (Matthew 10:8). His resurrection virtue is our spiritual endowment to advance His kingdom through creative conventions that defy the natural and spiritual problems in life.

Reigning in heaven to enlarge the kingdom

The reign of a king is to hold a royal office and rule over a domain. There is not a high office in all the Earth that is greater than being seated with King Jesus in heaven. Effectively reigning from our heavenly office requires a constant abiding in the King of kings (1 Timothy 6:15).

Reigning in heaven involves dedication to the kingdom virtue of Jesus to effectively rule in His kingdom on Earth. The kingdom virtues of righteousness, peace, and joy spiritually strengthen us to remain oriented in our royal place above. Our morally right standing with Jesus emboldens us to confidently claim our royal inheritance. As coheirs of Jesus, peace and joy empowers us to lay hold of our kingdom inheritance for a spiritually rich life (Romans 8:17).

The exercise of reigning from heaven is the personal application of kingdom virtues on Earth through the Holy Spirit. The Holy Spirit is our kingdom guide. Jesus explained the role of the Holy Spirit as, "the Spirit of truth, whom the world can not receive, because it does not see Him or know Him, but you know Him because He abides with you and will be in you" (John 14:17). The Spirit of truth leads us into the reality of the kingdom wherever we are in the world. He abides with us, teaching us, step by step, how to reach out to the world with the King's riches.

The Holy Spirit also increases our resolve to reign from heaven when faced with challenges in the world. Jesus prepared us for trials stating, "These things I have spoken to you, so that in Me you may have peace. In the world you have tribulation, but take courage; I have overcome the world" (John 16:33). The Holy Spirit, who is with us in both good and bad times, directs us through trials to bring out the best in us as an overcomer in Jesus. The ultimate purpose for trials is to prove our personal claim of being a follower of Jesus.

Our personal claim of being a follower of Jesus

Trouble from the world is not punishment from our heavenly Father. The absolute care of our Father to work all trials out for our good significantly points out the value He has placed on our life. Apostle Paul celebrated how the Father's hand is at work in all the events of our life declaring, "And we know that God causes all things to work together for good to those who love God, to those who are called according to His purpose" (Romans 8:28). Our Father carefully watches over us to develop what He has placed inside of us. Most importantly, He is interested in how we live up to our personal claim of love toward Him.

Our personal claim of love toward God must not be taken for granted. It encompasses who we are as a person in Jesus and the type of seated place we have in the kingdom. Our personal claim is something to be put on trial for in the world to defend our witness of the heavenly kingdom.

Jesus claimed He was the Son of God and came from God. He also declared that He would endure great suffering to fulfill God's plan for His life to the benefit of a dying world. Jesus was put on trial and put to death for standing firm in His personal claim. He defended His witness of His participation in the heavenly kingdom until His death.

Apostle Paul claimed to be an apostle that was seated in Jesus with the full authority of the apostolic office. When his high calling was put into question, He used his personal history of trials and suffering as proof of his apostleship from heaven.

Our personal claim from heaven is no less important than that of Jesus or the Apostle Paul. It is one of the most valuable kingdom assets in our life that helps us make the greatest impact in the lives of others. In short, our heavenly claim is a declaration to the world of our kingdom reality in Jesus.

Due to the process of spiritual growth, a personal claim will evolve over time. It will become a dynamic expression of a multi dimensionally developed identity over time. Every dimension of our identity will enhance our personal claim and enrich what we do to further our personal kingdom initiatives.

For instance, Jesus fulfills the finished work of the cross when we personally claim to be crucified with Him. Personally claiming to be crucified with Jesus gives believers a tremendous advantage over trespassing evil spirits. Identifying with Jesus as a crucified one, while renouncing a specific sin, removes legal ground for a spirit to keep trespassing in our life. Authoritatively telling spirits about their past defeat through the death of Jesus on the cross reminds them of their immediate defeat when telling them to leave. The finished work of the cross is executed when Jesus removes trespassing spirits that were already disarmed during His crucifixion about two thousand years ago.

In similar fashion, the Father backs our personal claim of being a seated one in heaven as we go to our school, work place, or market place. The Father creates a kingdom space within every context of life to enlarge His kingdom on Earth. He is simply waiting on us to proactively enter every environment from our position in Jesus to carry out the full implication of being a seated one in heaven.

Still, over time, our personal claim will become more individualized to the specific purpose the Father has created for us to serve. Our distinct kingdom influence will dramatically impact the world as we mature in our unique personal calling of being a royal heir of Jesus.

Collaborate with Jesus

Jesus desires to reveal Himself where we are in our relationship with Him right now, not after we theologically understand the Bible in its entirety. He said concerning Himself, "I am the way, and the truth, and the life. No one comes to the Father except through Me" (John 14:6). The way to the Father is a Person. Truth is a Person. Our new life is in a Person named Jesus.

Jesus has not insisted that we come to Him through a complete understanding of His written communication before we can experience an intimately personal connection with Him. It is necessary to learn all of the teachings of Jesus because His message gives us life to live through Him. Furthermore, His doctrine forms the foundation we are to base our lives on. However, Jesus is as relationally driven as He is doctrinally determined to bring us higher into Himself as the Truth.

Our life message

A kingdom education for every follower of Jesus involves developing a personal life message through a strong relationship with Him, as well as excelling in the application of His written word. Jesus is committed to making our life a living message of what it means to collaborate with Him.

A life message is not to be confused with a workplace mission statement or a religious doctrinal creed. Our career and denominational allegiances offer great input for our life message, but is not meant to replace it.

Our life message is the central theme and significant communication we send to the world with every action and word from our life. It is also the prevailing good news we preach to others through our behavior and lifestyle without using words. For this reason, it is vitally important that our behavior and lifestyle mirrors what we claim to believe in order to consistently express our authentic life message.

Since our life is above in Jesus, as we abide in Him, our life message will communicate the central theme of the Father's kingdom on Earth. Our significant communication to the world through everything we do and say is the good news of supernatural love and life through Jesus.

Father's high virtue in connection with the supermoral, self-denying, resurrection and kingdom virtues of Jesus gives deeper meaning to our life message. We live because of His breath in us. We give because He first gave to us. Our kingdom cause, supermorals, convictions, creative conventions and personal claim directs our purpose of being a sent one into the world. Meaning and purpose gives our life message supernatural substance that may influence others to believe in God for themselves.

Amplifying our voice

Our life message is heard by others through our voice. Voice is defined as an agency by which a particular point of view is expressed or represented (*New Oxford American Dictionary*). Our voice is the multifaceted expression of our life message through words, actions, and means of communicating our point of view.

We have to know how to accurately hear Jesus to develop our voice. One benefit of implementing a personal vision, mission, and values is to hear Jesus more clearly. A vision is a picture of the kind of future we will create with Jesus. A personal mission statement will immediately set in motion our own form of kingdom advocacy and/or establish steps toward a long-term personal undertaking. It is also advantageous to choose four or five personal core values that highlight key qualities in our spiritual makeup. Core values further develop our kingdom point of view and amplifies our voice when we fully live them out.

We have to experience Jesus as our life to develop our voice through behavior and lifestyle. The core kingdom competencies of prophesying, healing the sick, and casting out demons is part of the spiritual makeup of every believer. Jesus endued us with super-natural ability and power to communicate a kingdom point of view through a supernatural kingdom lifestyle.

The greatest miracle anyone can experience is the recreation of their dead spirit into a living spirit when asking Jesus to be their life. Still, demonstrating supernatural works before an unbeliever's life will catch their attention in ways that words cannot. In doing so, supernatural works done in love may possibly open their heart to the love of the Father.

Lastly, it is best for us to not rule out the simple forms of exercising our voice. A word of mouth *Collaborate Move•Meant* may ignite out of a simple discussion between two individuals over coffee. A form of advocacy may be sparked by a random act of kindness. Even something as common as T-shirt designs can start out as an inspiration and build up to become a personal enterprise over time. Regardless of the means, whether the opportunity involves money or not, we were sent into the world by our Father to communicate His heart with our unique voice.

Be it, outreach to people in the marketplace, public speaking, or a blog, it is important to immediately take ownership of the God-given call on our life. Although it will take time to fully develop our voice and operate in our calling, we can take disciplined steps toward our assigned place in the kingdom as soon as possible.

A well thought out kingdom vision and personal mission statement is a great place to begin. When we stretch our mind around a personal kingdom vision and take the time to work it out on paper, we will strengthen our voice for clear communication. Additionally, when we prayerfully seek God about the vision He has for our life, we will be less susceptible to settling for one we were never meant to own.

When a prophet of old inquired of God, He answered by saying, "Record the vision And inscribe it on tablets, That the one who reads it may run" (Habakkuk 2:2). A written vision will not only help us run, it will also help others run as well. When more than one person runs with a vision, the creation of a *Collaborate Move•Meant* will amplify every participants voice and further advance the kingdom of God.

Encounter with Jesus

As collaborators with Jesus, we have a heavenly call to live and love for the Father's glory. Fortunately, we are not observed from heaven, expected to expand the kingdom without the direct initiation and participation of the Father, Son, and Holy Spirit.

Our relationship with Jesus will deepen when we persistently search out our distinct identity and purpose in Him. He will give us kingdom downloads when we press into Him. Kingdom downloads will upgrade our sent profile for a more detailed kingdom vision. They will also upgrade our spiritual gift set to implement the vision more effectively through the Holy Spirit.

In conclusion, below is an updated sent profile with the kingdom upgrades previously mentioned in the *Collaborate Move•Meant* guide. Another testimony is provided to share how Jesus is committed to personally crown us with His love. Personal affirmations are also provided to bolster our faith as collaborators with Jesus. Regularly speaking the affirmations out loud over our life will fortify our hearts in the truth of God to live for His glory. Finally, more information is provided in the afterward for those who are interested in connecting with the *Collaborate Move•Meant* outreach.

My upgraded sent profile

- Kingdom cause I give my life for

- Supermorals I possess and live out

- Convictions I champion in the world

- Core abilities/creative conventions of Jesus I exercise

• Personal claim(s) I own

• Kingdom vision for advocacy/personal enterprise

• Kingdom mission for advocacy/personal enterprise

• Kingdom values for advocacy/personal enterprise

Concluding statement about the collaborative life I coauthor with the Father, Jesus, and the Holy Spirit.

Testimony

For about five months, a few of my friends and I met at the local Church in the morning before work. Michael and I alternated as the leader of the Bible study every Tuesday. The studies built on each other while each meeting usually complemented the previous one.

We decided to dub the second morning meeting of the week our encounter meetings. I was fortunate to be the one who directed the spontaneous activities as the Holy Spirit instructed. For only gathering about an hour each time, the meetings were spiritually rich and the unity between us was inspiring.

On one particular encounter meeting, Michael, Chris, Joey and I did prophetic activities inspired by Scripture and spontaneous declarations led by the Holy Spirit. We worshiped God and pressed into whatever He had in store for us that morning.

By the end of our meeting the Holy Spirit instructed me to have us stand side by side in front of the stage. Joey had left at that moment to go to work. I told Michael and Chris that God wanted to give us something. He wanted to celebrate who we were as individuals in the body of Jesus. We stood expectantly with our backs turned toward the stage.

I positioned myself to receive from God. A few minutes later I heard crying from my left side where Chris was standing. I looked over and saw Chris crying out loud while sitting on the stage. A little puzzled, I looked at Michael because Chris is one of those tough exterior type that you would not typically see crying.

I sat down beside Chris and asked if he was all right. He continued crying, so I just put my arm around his shoulders. Afterward, he proceeded to explain what had happened. He said that Jesus came to him and asked him to kneel before Him. Then, Jesus put a crown on his head and called him a king. Jesus also called Chris a diamond in the ruff, using language that personally spoke to his heart. While Chris was in astonishment from his personal encounter with Jesus, Michael and I praised God.

I believe the Holy Spirit paved the way for Chris to have an encounter with King Jesus. Even though we had Bible studies about Jesus and His kingdom, the Holy Spirit decided that was not enough. The Holy Spirit worked with us morning after morning during the encounter meetings so that the King of heaven could manifest the reality of the kingdom through a personal encounter.

Chris' coronation experience profoundly affected my life. I was changed within by the manifest presence and glory of Jesus. The demonstration of love from our King was my personal gift from God that memorable morning.

Prayer

Thank you Jesus, for proving how much you want to be my life. I am convinced you have done everything within your power to make a way for me to victoriously experience your life in every circumstance. I declare that in you I am an overcomer. Your love, peace, and life compel me to no longer live for myself.

Help me see the cross in your life. Help me grow in the judgment of the cross to choose your ways over the world's ways. I choose the life you have written for me in the story line of your sent paradigm, profile, and pattern.

Mature me in your ways to fully collaborate with you. Help me grow in my own personal sent vision for Father's glory. Thank you for crowning me with your love!

Personal affirmations

The word of God was life and spirit for Jesus while He followed the Father on Earth (John 6:63). Jesus is the living word of God that affirms and defends us now (John 1:1). Regularly speaking Biblical affirmations out loud over our life helps to powerfully engage the life and spirit of God's word with all of our being. As a result, the power of God's word is released to bring about personal transformation and tremendous circumstantial change.

Paradigm affirmations

Jesus lived on Earth by a heavenly paradigm. Jesus experienced God, the Father, as His life. He knew "the Father had given all things into His hands, and that He had come from God and was going to God"

(John 13:3). This same paradigm is now ours with Jesus as our life.

The Father has given all things into my hands, and I came from God and am going to God. (John 13:3)

For I have come down from heaven, not to do my own will, but the will of Him who sent me. (John 6:38)

If I speak from myself I seek my own glory; but when I seek the glory of the One who sent me I am true. (John 7:18)

If I honor myself, my honor is nothing. It is my Father who honors me. (John 8:54)

"I can do nothing of myself; but as my Father taught me, I speak these things. And He who sent me is with me. The Father has not left me alone, for I always do those things that please Him". (John 8:28-29)

Profile affirmations of our new person in Jesus

I have received Jesus and have been given the power to become a son/daughter of the Father because I believe in His name. (John 1:12)

I am a citizen of heaven. (Philippians 3:20)

In Jesus dwells all the fullness of the Godhead and I am complete in Him. (Colossians 2:9-10)

I am more than a conqueror through Jesus who loves me. (Romans 8:37)

Jesus was made to be sin on my behalf so that I might become the righteousness of God in Him. (2 Corinthians 5:21)

I have become a king and priest to the Father and reign on Earth through Jesus. (Revelation 5:10)

Profile affirmations of our new possessions in Jesus

I am blessed with every spiritual blessing in the heavenly places in Christ. (Ephesians 1:3)

His divine power has given to me all things that pertain to life and godliness, through the knowledge of Him who called me by glory and virtue. (2 Peter 1:3)

Profile affirmations of our new position in Jesus

I am crucified with Jesus. (Galatians 2:20)

I am seated with Jesus in the heavenly places. (Ephesians 2:4-6)

Profile affirmations of our new plan in Jesus

My Father chose me in Him before the foundation of the world that I should be holy and without blame before Him in love, having predestined me to adoption as a son/ daughter by Jesus Christ to Himself, according to the good pleasure of His will, to the praise of the glory of His grace, by which He made me accepted in the Beloved. (Ephesians 1:4-6)

I will not be conformed to this world. I will be transformed by the renewing of my mind so that I prove what God's will is for my life. (Romans 12:2)

Notes

_____

_____

_____

_____

_____

_____

_____

_____

_____

_____

Sent pattern affirmations

Coming from heaven
to manifest the Father's love

But God, who is rich in mercy, made me alive together with Christ (by grace I have been saved), and raised me up together, and made me sit together in the heavenly places in Christ Jesus. (Ephesians 2:4-6)

Orienting in Jesus to live from heaven

I have been raised up with Christ. I keep seeking the things above, where Christ is, seated at the right hand of God. I set my mind on the things above, not on the things that are on the Earth. I have died and my life is hidden with Christ in God. When Christ who is my life, is revealed, then I also will be revealed with Him in glory. (Colossians 3:1-4)

Dying to self-oriented life through the cross

I have been crucified with Christ; it is no longer I who live, but Christ lives in me; and the life which I now live in the flesh I live by the faith of the Son of God, who loved me and gave Himself for me. (Galatians 2:20)

Experiencing resurrection life for the Father's glory

I have been buried with Jesus through baptism into death, that just as Christ was raised from the dead by the glory of the Father, even so I should walk in newness of life. (Romans 6:4)

Reigning from heaven to enlarge the kingdom

I am sent from heaven just as the Father sent Jesus to fulfill His commission on Earth. (John 17:18)

I receive the peace of Jesus. He has sent me just as the Father has sent Him. (John 20:21)

Notes

_____

_____

_____

_____

_____

_____

_____

_____

Sent profile upgrades

Coming from heaven to manifest the Father's love/Kingdom cause

The kingdom cause will be worth giving our life for even though it may not be fulfilled within our lifetime. (Pg. 62)

A higher morality/Supermoral lifestyle

We learn how to supermorally conduct ourselves to supernaturally benefit others. (Pg. 68)

Dying to self-centered life through the cross/Conviction

We die to ourself to champion our conviction in the world. (Pg. 70)

Experiencing resurrection life for the Father's glory/Creative conventions

The creative conventions of doing miracles, signs, and wonders become part of our lifestyle. (Pg. 73)

Our personal claim of being a follower of Jesus/Heavenly personal claim

A personal claim is something to be put on trial for in the world to defend our witness of the heavenly kingdom. (Pg. 75)

Notes

Notes

Notes

_____

_____

_____

_____

_____

_____

_____

_____

_____

_____

_____

_____

_____

_____

_____

_____

_____

_____

Notes

Notes

_____

_____

_____

_____

_____

_____

_____

_____

_____

_____

_____

_____

_____

_____

_____

AFTERWORD

The *Collaborate Move•Meant* guide was written to expressly declare, "God meant for Jesus to move us." An outreach called, *Collaborate Move•Meant*, was also created to proclaim the aforementioned watchword through an organized undertaking. Check out the website for more information pertaining to the *Collaborate Move•Meant* guide and outreach.

Thank you for reading the *Collaborate Move•Meant* guide. As a final word, always remember where you are seated and do not let anyone cheat you of your crown (Revelation 3:11).

Jesus collaborator,

Donovan Dreyfus
collaboratemovemeant.com
facebook.com/CollaborateMoveMeant

ENDNOTES

New Oxford American Dictionary, 2nd Edition. Copyright © 2005. Used for all dictionary references.

Sozo ministry is the inner healing and deliverance program of Bethel Church in Redding California. http://www.bethelredding.com

Ana Méndez Ferrell, *Eat my Body, Drink my Blood.* Copyright © 2006. http://www.voiceofthelight.com

Unless otherwise noted, all scripture references are taken from the New American Standard Bible Copyright © 1960, 1962, 1963, 1968, 1971, 1972, 1973, 1975, 1977, 1995 by The Lockman Foundation, La Habra, California. Used by permission. All rights reserved.

All Biblical references with NKJV following stands for the New King James version of the Bible. Scripture taken from the New King James Version®. Copyright © 1982 by Thomas Nelson, Inc. Used by permission. All rights reserved.

HOLY BIBLE, King James Version, Cambridge Edition, Galatians 2:20.

Collaborate Method

Do you have an interest in starting a Church or upgrading the ministry model of an existing one? Donovan Dreyfus created the Collaborate Method to assist new Church startups and established Churches in reaching their full potential for the kingdom of God. Visit collaboratemethod.com for more information about this innovative approach to ministry based on the Collaborate Move•Meant guide.

Startup Prayer

Do you have a passion for prayer? Connect with others who also commit to prayer at the official Startup Prayer Facebook page and on Twitter.

Open Blue Church

Donovan Dreyfus started Open Blue Church with a unique vision to unconditionally invest in the personal God-given calling of believers. Check out openbluechurch.com for more information about this new pioneering Church startup.

open
blue
church
(live sent from above)

collaborate
move·meant
God meant for Jesus to move us

Made in the USA
Middletown, DE
09 July 2017